barbecues and salads

THE AUSTRALIAN
Women's Weekly

contents

For weekends and the long nights of summer, there is nothing better than the waft of food cooking outside on a barbecue. It's a great way to cook: instead of using fats, marinated meat or fish is tender, hugely tasty and very healthy! Then to accompany your great tasting barbecued food, add one of these salads – choose your leaves carefully, then add lots of great combinations for the perfect meal!

Food Director

Pamela Clark

barbecuing

The backyard barbecue has come a long way from the days when Dad donned an apron and charred some sausages. Now the barbecue is an indispensable part of summer life – and with instant gas and electric barbecues, some people barbecue every single night. It's cleaner than cooking in the kitchen, uses fewer pans, and it feels healthy and relaxed standing on the balcony or terrace turning the prawns with your tongs while your partner makes the salad. And once it's over there's not much to do in the way of a clean up.

choosing the barbecue

Barbecues come in two types: covered and uncovered. A covered barbecue is the most useful because you can use it as an oven with the cover closed or as a traditional barbecue with the cover open. Small covered barbecues can be used on a terrace or balcony. If you normally entertain on a large scale however, you'll probably need a large fixed barbecue. If your barbecue is only used for quickly-cooked steaks, chops, fish and sausages, a portable uncovered barbecue might be all you need.

covered barbecues

Also called kettle barbecues (the most well-known is the Weber) they can be powered by gas or charcoal. They have a domed lid with air vents top and bottom. Cold air passes up through the bottom vents, providing oxygen to keep the coals burning, and swirls around in the barbecue, giving the food its characteristic smoky flavour, then leaves through the top vents. It works in the same way as a convection oven, the heat is reflected off the lid giving you two sources of heat so you can cook whole birds, ham and roasts. Uncover the barbecue to cook steaks, sausages and chops.

fixed barbecues

These are constructions usually made of brick which are built in the backyard. Their disadvantage is that they can't be moved if it rains but their advantage is that you can

Begin cooking when coals look like this

build them as big as you like with flat plates, grills and food preparation areas. If you entertain a lot in your backyard, especially for big gatherings, a fixed barbecue is often your best bet. You can use wood or charcoal on fixed barbecues.

portable uncovered barbecues
From tiny Hibachis to big wagon barbecues, you can buy gas or charcoal-powered varieties. They are on castors for easy mobility and many come with grills and flat plates They also have side flaps for bench space, and often a shelf underneath for storage.

the fuel
Barbecues can be fuelled by wood, charcoal, gas or electricity.
Wood requires pieces of various sizes, kindling and paper. Allow wood to char before cooking and never use treated wood on a barbecue. Move food away from extreme heat to prevent burning.
Charcoal is made from hardwood or lumpwood. It lights quickly, burns with twice the heat of heat beads and smells cleaner. Heat beads or briquettes are made from ground charcoal, coal dust and starch. For direct cooking, one layer of charcoal should cover an area slightly larger than the food. For indirect cooking, use twice the depth of coals as they need to burn longer. Place charcoal or heat beads in a mound and insert two or three firelighters among them. Don't attempt to cook anything while the firelighters are burning or your food will taste of kerosene. Allow the coals to burn down until they're covered with grey ash (about 30 minutes), spread them out, then start cooking. To increase heat, tap coals with metal tongs to remove accumulated ash, push the coals closer together, then open all vents and add more charcoal. To lessen the heat, partially close the vents and push the coals further apart.

Gas or electric barbecues are faster and will heat up in about 15 minutes. Gas barbecues come with a gas bottle and electric barbecues require a nearby power source. Most models have heat controls and at least two burners so you can cook different foods simultaneously. They work by heating either Lava or ceramic rocks. Lava rocks can be removed, washed then dried in the sun before replacing them in the barbecue. Ceramic rocks are non-porous and contain lava rock. To clean, turn them upside-down and allow the gas burners to burn off any residue. Most gas barbecues have a slide-out draining tray which should be lined with foil and sprinkled evenly with fat absorber. Replace this, and the grease receptacle, regularly as accumulated fat and grease can cause flare-ups.
Fit a gasfuse between the cylinder bottle and the regulator to prevent gas leaks and possible disastrous explosions.

cleaning the barbecue
All barbecues should be cleaned after use. It's much easier to clean a still-warm barbecue than a cold food-encrusted one. A gas barbecue should be turned on to high and when the grill or plate begins to smoke, turn the gas off at the bottle (to prevent gas build-up in the hose), then at the controls.

For all types of barbecues use a stiff wire brush and cold water (no detergent) to scrub the grill and plate. Lightly spray or brush the grill with light vegetable oil before putting it away, to prevent rusting.

If your barbecue can't be moved out of the rain, invest in a cover to protect it from rust. Ash from wood or charcoal barbecues should be allowed to cool down, then it can be spread evenly over the garden. If you have a small garden and barbecue frequently, this will clearly not be a solution for long. Place the cooled ash in a plastic bag and discard.

setting up the barbecue

indirect heat

This is used in a covered barbecue. With gas, the food is placed in a preheated covered barbecue. The burners directly under the food are turned off while the side burners remain on. With a charcoal barbecue, metal bars hold two stacks of

Indirect heat uses a disposable aluminium baking dish

Direct heat is the traditional method of barbecuing

coals against the barbecue's sides leaving the centre of the barbecue rack empty. A disposable aluminium baking dish can be placed here for fat drips, if desired.

direct heat

This is the traditional method, where the food is placed on the barbecue grill or plate and cooked directly over the heat source. It is the best method for sausages, steaks, burgers and vegetables. A rotisserie may be used with direct cooking over low burners (gas) or with an enamel baking dish below the roast (charcoal) to minimise flare-ups. Food can also be wrapped in foil to protect it when using direct heat.

combination heat

If you have a covered barbecue you can use a combination of both methods. Thick steaks or pieces of chicken, for instance, can be seared first, using direct heat, then covered and cooked using indirect heat for more even cooking and juice retention.

smoking

Smoking is a cooking stye in which the flavours of the food are affected by the choice of wood used. Hickory and mesquite are the best known woods for smoking, but there are many different varieties available, such as applewood, tea tree, cherry, peach or banksia. Wood chips have to be soaked first in cold water so that they will smoulder slowly over the fire, rather than burn. For additonal flavours and scents, soak a variety of herbs and spices in the water along with the wood chips. Smoking is best suited to moderate-to-slow cooking. Instead of placing the soaked wood chips and herbs directly onto the open flame where they burn too rapidly, put them in a smoke box to combust slowly without causing flare-ups. During preheating, place the filled cast-iron smoke box over the heat source. When smoke appears from within the box, adjust the burners on a gas barbecue to low. If using a charcoal barbecue, place the smoke box directly under the food and use indirect heat. For the best results when smoking try not to interrupt cooking by frequently opening the lid for basting.

useful tips

herb flavours

When you prune your bay tree or rosemary bush, save the clippings and toss them on the fire before cooking. The flavours of the herbs will permeate the dish – excellent with meat, fish and vegetables.

preheating the barbecue

A gas barbecue should only take 10 to 15 minutes to heat up but a charcoal or wood fired barbecue might take up to 1 hour.

cooking fish in newspaper

This is a very good way to barbecue whole oily fish such as salmon. Stuff the cleaned fish with fresh herbs and slices of lemon, season with salt and pepper and rub the outside with a little olive oil. Wrap in lots of newspaper (a big section of a Sunday broadsheet) and tie securely with string. Thoroughly wet the newspaper and place it on the barbecue, turning once. It will take about 1 hour, depending on the weight of the fish. Make sure the fish is skinned before eating.

safety with barbecues

Always keep a spray bottle filled with water handy to douse flare-ups. It will not affect the food being cooked on gas barbecues but will cause ash to rise and settle on the food when cooking with wood or charcoal, so only use as a last resort in this case.

cooking times

These are to be used a guide only as the time can vary depending on the type of barbecue used.

meat thermometers

Use a meat thermometer to determine cooking time for larger cuts of meat, but never leave the thermometer in the meat while it's cooking. Insert it towards the end of the cooking time and leave in for a few minutes or until the temperature stabilises.

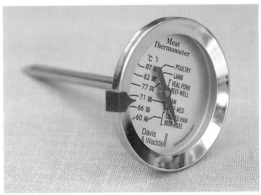

rare, medium and well-done

Try not to cut into a steak to see if it is ready – you'll lose juices that way. Instead, press the surface of the steak with tongs. Rare steak is soft to the touch; the outside is cooked and brown, the inside is red. Medium steak is firm to the touch, well browned on the outside and pink in the centre. Well-done steak is very firm to the touch, browned on the outside and evenly cooked through the centre, but not dry.

seafood skewers with radicchio & fennel salad

8 uncooked large king prawns (560g)
8 cleaned baby octopus (720g)
400g firm white fish fillets
8 scallops (200g), roe removed
2 teaspoons fennel seeds
2 teaspoons dried green peppercorns
2 tablespoons white wine vinegar
2 cloves garlic, crushed
1 tablespoon olive oil
2 medium radicchio (400g)
2 small fennel bulbs (400g), trimmed,
    sliced thinly
1 cup firmly packed fresh flat-leaf parsley
    leaves

mustard dressing
¼ cup (60ml) white wine vinegar
½ teaspoon mustard powder
1 tablespoon olive oil
1 teaspoon sugar
4 spring onions, chopped coarsely

1 Shell and devein prawns, leaving tails intact. Remove heads and beaks from octopus. Cut fish into 2.5cm pieces. Combine seafood in large bowl.

2 Using mortar and pestle, crush seeds and peppercorns coarsely, add to seafood with vinegar, garlic and oil; toss gently to combine. Cover; refrigerate 3 hours or overnight.

3 Make mustard dressing.

4 Thread seafood, alternating varieties, on skewers; cook on heated barbecue or lightly oiled grill plate until seafood is just changed in colour and cooked as desired.

5 Meanwhile, discard dark outer leaves of radicchio, tear inner leaves roughly. Combine radicchio in medium bowl with fennel, parsley and dressing; toss gently to combine. Serve seafood skewers on salad.

mustard dressing Place ingredients in screw-top jar; shake well.

preparation time 25 minutes (plus marinating time)
cooking time 10 minutes
serves 4
per serving 13.9g fat; 2082kJ (498 cal)
tips Any firm white fish fillet can be used in this recipe.
Use green peppercorns in brine if you can't find the dried variety; rinse then drain them thoroughly before using.
You will need to soak eight bamboo skewers in water for at least an hour before use to prevent splintering and scorching.

cajun fish cutlets with lime

2 teaspoons ground cumin
2 teaspoons ground coriander
2 teaspoons sweet paprika
2 teaspoons mustard powder
2 teaspoons onion powder
½ teaspoon garlic powder
¼ teaspoon cayenne pepper
2 teaspoons fennel seeds
4 white fish cutlets (1kg)
2 limes, sliced thickly

1 Combine spices, powders, pepper and seeds with fish in large bowl. Coat fish all over in spice mixture.
2 Cook fish, in batches, on heated oiled grill plate or barbecue until browned both sides and cooked as desired.
3 Meanwhile, cook lime on same grill plate or barbecue until browned both sides.
4 Divide fish among serving plates; top with slices of lime.

preparation time 10 minutes
cooking time 10 minutes
serves 4
per serving 5.9g fat; 1078kJ (258 cal)
tips Any firm white fish can be used in this recipe. You can use ⅓ cup bottled cajun spice mix, available from supermarkets, instead of making your own, if preferred.

fish cutlets with pesto butter

60g butter
2 tablespoons basil pesto
¼ teaspoon cracked black pepper
1 teaspoon finely grated lemon rind
4 white fish cutlets (1kg)
100g baby spinach leaves, trimmed

1   Blend or process butter, pesto, pepper and rind in small bowl until well combined.
2   Cook fish, in batches, on heated oiled grill plate or barbecue until browned and cooked as desired.
3   Top fish with pesto butter; cook until butter melts.
4   Serve with baby spinach leaves and, if desired, slices of lemon.

preparation time 10 minutes
cooking time 10 minutes
serves 4
per serving 24.5g fat; 1584kJ (379 cal)
tip Any firm white fish can be used in this recipe.

lime-marinated fish cutlets with tomato & onion salsa

1 clove garlic, crushed
1 tablespoon finely grated lime rind
2 tablespoons oyster sauce
½ cup (125ml) sweet chilli sauce
½ cup (125ml) lime juice
4 white fish cutlets (1kg)
2 medium tomatoes (380g), deseeded, chopped finely
1 medium red onion (170g), chopped finely

1 Combine garlic, rind, oyster sauce and 1/3 cup each of the chilli sauce and juice in large bowl; add fish. Cover; refrigerate 1 hour.
2 Meanwhile, combine tomato, onion, remaining chilli sauce and remaining juice in small bowl. Cover; refrigerate until required.
3 Drain fish; reserve marinade.
4 Cook fish on heated oiled barbecue, uncovered, until browned both sides and just cooked through, brushing occasionally with reserved marinade during cooking.
5 Serve fish topped with tomato and onion salsa.

preparation time 20 minutes (plus marinating time)
cooking time 10 minutes
serves 4
per serving 6.3g fat; 1308kJ (312 cal)
tip Any firm white fish can be used in this recipe.

tuna with
mixed vegetable stir-fry

¼ cup (60ml) sweet chilli sauce
¼ cup (60ml) lime juice
1 tablespoon chopped fresh coriander
6 tuna steaks (1.2kg)
2 tablespoons finely grated lime rind
1 small fresh red thai chilli, deseeded,
    chopped finely
1 clove garlic, crushed
2 medium courgettes (240g)
2 medium carrots (240g)
2 medium red peppers (400g),
    sliced thinly
1 medium yellow pepper (200g),
    sliced thinly
1 small red onion (100g), sliced thinly

1 Combine sauce, 2 teaspoons of the juice and coriander in small bowl.

2 Combine remaining juice in large bowl with tuna, rind, chilli and garlic. Cover; refrigerate 1 hour.

3 Meanwhile, cut courgettes and carrots into very thin slices lengthways; cut slices into matchstick-sized pieces.

4 Drain tuna; cook, in batches, on heated oiled grill plate or barbecue until browned and cooked as desired.

5 Meanwhile, heat oiled wok or large non-stick frying pan; cook 1 tablespoon of the chilli sauce mixture, courgettes, carrot, peppers and onion, in batches, until vegetables are just tender.

6 Serve tuna on vegetables, drizzled with remaining chilli sauce mixture.

preparation time 10 minutes (plus marinating time)
cooking time 10 minutes
serves 6
per serving 12g fat; 1517kJ (363 cal)
tip Tuna is best when both sides have been seared and the centre is fairly rare; overcooking can render this fish dry and unpalatable.

tuna with olive salsa

6 tuna steaks (1kg)
½ cup (125ml) olive oil
¼ cup (60ml) lemon juice
2 cloves garlic, crushed
4 medium tomatoes (360g), quartered
50g baby spinach leaves

olive salsa
200g pitted kalamata olives,
   chopped finely
⅓ cup (50g) drained, coarsely
   chopped capers
2 tablespoons finely grated lemon rind
½ cup coarsely chopped fresh
   flat-leaf parsley
¼ cup coarsely chopped fresh oregano

1 Place tuna in shallow dish; pour over combined oil, juice and garlic. Cover; refrigerate 1 hour.
2 Drain tuna; discard marinade.
3 Cook tuna and tomato on heated oiled barbecue, uncovered, until tuna is browned both sides and cooked as desired, and tomato is tender.
4 Serve tuna with tomato, olive salsa and spinach.

olive salsa Combine ingredients in small bowl.

preparation time 15 minutes (plus marinating time)
cooking time 10 minutes
serves 6
per serving 22.2g fat; 1726kJ (412 cal)

swordfish steaks with tomato & chilli butter

6 swordfish steaks (1.2kg)
1 teaspoon grated lime rind
¼ cup (60ml) lime juice

tomato and chilli butter
125g butter
⅓ cup (50g) drained, finely chopped
    sun-dried tomatoes
1 tablespoon lime juice
1 tablespoon sambal oelek
1 tablespoon finely chopped fresh
    flat-leaf parsley

1 Combine fish, rind and juice in large shallow dish.
Cover; refrigerate 30 minutes.
2 Drain fish; discard marinade.
3 Cook fish on heated oiled barbecue, uncovered,
until browned both sides and just cooked through.
4 Serve with tomato and chilli butter.

tomato and chilli butter Beat butter in small bowl
with electric mixer until light and fluffy; add tomato,
juice, sambal oelek and parsley. Spoon mixture onto
greaseproof paper or foil. Roll up firmly; shape into
log. Refrigerate 1 hour or until firm.

preparation time 20 minutes (plus marinating
and refrigeration time)
cooking time 10 minutes
serves 6
per serving 22.3g fat; 1608kJ (384 cal)
tip Tomato and chilli butter can be made a week
ahead and refrigerated, covered.

nutty rice snapper

2kg whole snapper

stuffing
60g butter
1 medium brown onion (150g),
    chopped finely
2 cloves garlic, crushed
1 tablespoon ground coriander
1 tablespoon ground cumin
2 teaspoons mustard powder
2 teaspoons sweet paprika
2 teaspoons mild curry powder
2 cups cooked long grain rice
½ cup (75g) pistachios, toasted
2 tablespoons coarsely chopped
    fresh flat-leaf parsley
2 tablespoons coarsely chopped
    fresh coriander leaves
2 teaspoons finely grated lemon rind

1 Score fish three times on each side.
2 Fill cavity of the fish with stuffing; wrap in lightly oiled foil.
3 Place fish on heated oiled barbecue; cook, covered, using indirect heat, following manufacturer's instructions, about 1 hour or until cooked through.

stuffing Melt butter in medium frying pan; cook onion and garlic until onion is soft. Add spices; cook, stirring, until fragrant. Combine onion mixture, rice, nuts, herbs and rind in large bowl.

preparation time 20 minutes
cooking time 1 hour 10 minutes
serves 8
per serving 14.6g fat; 1687kJ (403 cal)
tip You will need to cook about ¾ cup (150g) rice for this recipe.

swordfish with olive paste

200g kalamata olives, pitted
¼ cup (50g) drained capers
⅓ cup finely chopped fresh dill
⅓ cup finely chopped fresh flat-leaf
   parsley
2 cloves garlic, crushed
2 tablespoons lemon juice
4 swordfish steaks (800g)

1 Blend or process olives, capers, dill, parsley, garlic and juice until mixture forms an almost smooth paste.
2 Cook fish on heated oiled barbecue, uncovered, until browned both sides and just cooked through. Spread olive paste over fish to serve.

preparation time 15 minutes
cooking time 10 minutes
serves 4
per serving 5g fat; 1067kJ (255 cal)
tip Olive paste can be made 3 days ahead and refrigerated, covered.

prawns with garlic & caper butter

24 large uncooked prawns (1kg)
80g butter
4 cloves garlic, crushed
1 tablespoon drained baby capers,
   chopped coarsely
1 tablespoon chopped fresh oregano

1 Peel prawns, leaving tails intact. To butterfly prawns, cut halfway through the back, remove vein, then press flat.
2 Melt butter in small saucepan; add garlic, capers and oregano. Remove from heat.
3 Cook prawns on heated, oiled grill plate or barbecue until browned on one side; turn, spoon over some of the butter mixture, cook until just cooked through.
4 Serve with remaining butter mixture.

preparation time 20 minutes
cooking time 10 minutes
serves 4
per serving 17.2g fat; 1091kJ
(261 cal)

prawn skewers
with lime & spring onions

36 medium uncooked prawns (1.5kg)
2 tablespoons lime juice
2 tablespoons olive oil
2 cloves garlic, crushed
3 spring onions

1 Peel and devein prawns leaving tails intact.
2 Combine prawns, lime juice, oil and garlic in large bowl.
3 Cut spring onions into 4cm lengths. Thread three prawns onto each of 12 skewers, threading a piece of spring onion after each prawn.
4 Cook skewers on heated oiled barbecue or grill plate until browned on both sides and just cooked through.

preparation time 25 minutes
cooking time 10 minutes
serves 4
per serving 10.4g fat; 1078kJ (258 cal)
tips The prawns can be marinated in lime mixture for up to 1 hour. If you are using metal skewers, oil them first to prevent the prawns sticking. And don't forget, they will be very hot after cooking. If using bamboo skewers, it is best to soak them in water for at least an hour before using.

coconut prawns with turmeric coriander mayonnaise

1kg large uncooked prawns
2 eggs, beaten lightly
1 cup (70g) shredded coconut
6 potato roti (or chapattis), to serve

turmeric coriander mayonnaise

¼ teaspoon ground turmeric
2 tablespoons boiling water
1 clove garlic, crushed
2 teaspoons finely grated lemon rind
½ cup (150g) mayonnaise
2 tablespoons finely chopped fresh
    coriander

1 Peel and devein prawns, leaving tails intact.
2 Dip prawns in egg; coat in coconut.
3 Cook prawns on heated oiled barbecue plate,
uncovered, until browned and cooked through.
4 Cook roti on heated oiled barbecue, uncovered,
until browned.
5 Serve prawns with turmeric coriander mayonnaise
and roti.

turmeric coriander mayonnaise Combine
ingredients in small bowl.

preparation time 30 minutes
cooking time 10 minutes
serves 4
per serving 27.6g fat; 2099kJ (501 cal)

prawn kebabs & chilli lime sauce

1kg medium uncooked prawns
2 cloves garlic, crushed
1 tablespoon finely chopped fresh
   lemongrass
1 tablespoon balsamic vinegar
1 tablespoon coarsely chopped
   fresh coriander
1 tablespoon groundnut oil
4 spring onions

chilli lime sauce
⅔ cup (150g) sugar
½ cup (125ml) water
1 teaspoon finely grated lime rind
2 fresh red thai chillies, seeded,
   chopped finely
2 tablespoons sweet chilli sauce
⅓ cup (80ml) lime juice

1 Shell and devein prawns, leaving tails intact.
2 Combine garlic, lemongrass, vinegar, coriander and oil in large bowl; add prawns. Cover; refrigerate 3 hours or overnight.
3 Drain prawns; discard marinade.
4 Cut onions into 5cm lengths. Thread onion and prawns onto eight skewers.
5 Cook prawns on heated oiled barbecue, uncovered, until browned both sides and changed in colour. Serve with chilli lime sauce.

chilli lime sauce Combine sugar and the water in small saucepan; stir over heat, without boiling, until sugar dissolves. Simmer, uncovered, without stirring, 5 minutes. Add rind, chilli and sauce; simmer, uncovered, 5 minutes. Stir in juice; cool.

preparation time 40 minutes (plus marinating time)
cooking time 25 minutes (plus cooling time)
serves 4
per serving 5.7g fat; 1321kJ (316 cal)
tip If using bamboo skewers, soak in water for at least 1 hour before using, to avoid scorching.

portuguese chicken

1.6kg whole chicken
½ cup (125ml) lemon juice
2 tablespoons olive oil
4 fresh red thai chillies, deseeded,
    chopped finely
1 tablespoon brown sugar
1 tablespoon sweet paprika
1 clove garlic, crushed
2 teaspoons dried oregano
2 teaspoons salt

1 Rinse chicken under cold running water; pat dry with absorbent paper. Using kitchen scissors, cut along both sides of backbone; discard backbone. Place chicken, skin-side up, on board; using heel of hand, press down on breastbone to flatten chicken. Insert metal skewer through thigh and opposite wing of chicken to keep chicken flat. Repeat with other thigh and wing.
2 Place chicken in large shallow dish; pour over combined remaining ingredients. Cover; refrigerate 3 hours or overnight.
3 Drain chicken; reserve marinade.
4 Place chicken on oiled wire rack over disposable baking dish; pour over reserved marinade. Cook in covered barbecue, using indirect heat, following manufacturer's instructions, about 1¼ hours or until browned and cooked through, brushing occasionally with pan juices during cooking.
5 Serve with a crispy garden salad and crusty bread, if desired.

preparation time 15 minutes (plus marinating time)
cooking time 1 hour 15 minutes
serves 4
per serving 41.6g fat; 2288kJ (546 cal)

Poultry and barbecues are made for each other – golden sticky wings, marinated breasts threaded on skewers and flattened chicken halves in the incomparable Portuguese style. Other barbecued birds, such as quail and turkey, are just as delicious.

salt & pepper chicken skewers on baby pak choy

8 chicken thigh fillets (880g), chopped
    coarsely
1 teaspoon sichuan peppercorns,
    crushed
½ teaspoon five-spice powder
2 teaspoons sea salt
1 teaspoon sesame oil
600g baby pak choy, quartered
1 tablespoon oyster sauce
1 teaspoon soy sauce
1 tablespoon chopped fresh coriander

1 Thread chicken onto 12 skewers. Combine peppercorns, five-spice and salt in small bowl; sprinkle mixture over chicken, then press in firmly.
2 Cook chicken, in batches, on heated oiled grill plate or barbecue until browned and cooked through.
3 Meanwhile, heat oil in wok or large frying pan; stir-fry pak choy with the combined sauces until just wilted.
4 Divide pak choy among serving plates; top with chicken skewers. Serve sprinkled with coriander.

preparation time 15 minutes
cooking time 15 minutes
serves 4
per serving 17.4g fat; 1417kJ (339 cal)
tip You need 12 skewers for this recipe; if using bamboo skewers, soak them in water for an hour before use to prevent them from splintering or scorching.

chicken, lemon & artichoke skewers

3 medium lemons (420g)
¼ cup (60ml) olive oil
600g chicken breast fillets, chopped
2 x 400g cans artichoke hearts,
    drained, halved
24 button mushrooms

1 Squeeze juice from 1 lemon (you will need
2 tablespoons juice). Combine juice and oil in a jar
and shake well.
2 Cut remaining lemons into 24 wedges. Thread
chicken pieces, artichokes, mushrooms and lemon
onto 12 skewers.
3 Cook skewers on heated lightly oiled grill plate
or barbecue until browned all over and thoroughly
cooked through. Brush with oil mixture occasionally
during cooking.

preparation time 15 minutes
cooking time 15 minutes
serves 4
per serving 17.8g fat; 1417kJ
(339 cal)
tip This recipe can be prepared a
day ahead.

marinated chicken wings

1.5kg large chicken wings
1 cup (250ml) tomato sauce
½ cup (125ml) plum sauce
¼ cup (60ml) worcestershire sauce
¼ cup (50g) firmly packed brown sugar
2 cloves garlic, crushed

1 Cut wings into three pieces at joints; discard tips.
2 Combine remaining ingredients in large bowl; add chicken. Cover; refrigerate 3 hours or overnight.
3 Drain chicken; discard marinade.
4 Place chicken on oiled wire rack over disposable baking dish. Cook in covered barbecue, using indirect heat, following manufacturer's instructions, about 40 minutes or until browned and cooked through.

preparation time 20 minutes (plus marinating time)
cooking time 40 minutes
serves 6
per serving 24.3g fat; 1961kJ (468 cal)

tandoori chicken drumsticks

12 chicken drumsticks (1.8kg)
½ cup (140g) plain yogurt
2 teaspoons ground cumin
2 teaspoons ground coriander
1 teaspoon sweet paprika
2 cloves garlic, crushed
few drops red food colouring
½ cup (160g) lime pickle
½ cup (160g) mango chutney

1 Score chicken skin. Combine yogurt, spices, garlic and food colouring in large bowl; add chicken. Cover; refrigerate 3 hours or overnight.
2 Cook undrained chicken on heated oiled barbecue, uncovered, until browned and cooked through.
3 Serve chicken with pickle and chutney.

preparation time 10 minutes (plus marinating time)
cooking time 20 minutes
serves 4
per serving 40.7g fat; 2855kJ (682 cal)

five-spice chicken

750g chicken tenderloins
1 teaspoon groundnut oil
1½ teaspoons five-spice powder
2 cloves garlic, crushed
250g hokkien noodles
300g baby corn
500g asparagus
1 medium red pepper (200g),
   sliced thinly
¼ cup chopped fresh flat-leaf parsley

1 Combine chicken, oil, five-spice and garlic in medium bowl.
2 Cook chicken, in batches, on heated oiled grill plate or barbecue until browned and cooked through.
3 Meanwhile, place noodles in a heatproof bowl; cover with boiling water, separate with fork, drain.
4 Cut baby corn in half. Snap woody ends off asparagus; chop remaining spears into same-sized pieces as halved corn. Stir-fry corn, asparagus and pepper in heated lightly oiled wok or large frying pan until just tender; add noodles.
5 Stir parsley into vegetables off the heat, divide mixture among serving dishes and top with chicken.

preparation time 10 minutes
cooking time 15 minutes
serves 4
per serving 16.1g fat; 1647kJ (394 cal)

honey dijon chicken with creamy celery and fennel slaw

2 tablespoons honey
2 teaspoons dijon mustard
4 single chicken breast fillets (680g)

creamy fennel and celery slaw
2 medium fennel bulbs (600g)
3 trimmed celery stalks (300g),
  sliced thinly
¼ cup coarsely chopped fresh
  flat-leaf parsley
2 teaspoons dijon mustard
2 tablespoons lemon juice
2 tablespoons light soured cream
2 cloves garlic, crushed
¼ cup (75g) low-fat mayonnaise

1 Combine honey and mustard in small bowl. Brush chicken both sides with half of the honey mixture; cook, in batches, on lightly oiled heated barbecue about 15 minutes or until thoroughly cooked through, brushing occasionally with remaining honey mixture during cooking.
2 Meanwhile, make creamy fennel and celery slaw.
3 Serve chicken with slaw, sprinkled with reserved fennel tips.

creamy fennel and celery slaw Trim fennel, reserving about 1 tablespoon of the tips (discard the rest). Slice fennel thinly; combine with celery and parsley in large bowl. Combine remaining ingredients in small bowl, pour over slaw mixture; toss gently to combine.

preparation time 20 minutes
cooking time 30 minutes
serves 4
per serving 8.8g fat; 1371kJ (328 cal)

lemon basil chicken on hot potato salad

4 chicken thighs (640g)
2 cloves garlic, crushed
2 tablespoons lemon juice
1 teaspoon cracked black pepper
½ cup chopped fresh basil
5 slices pancetta (75g)
500g tiny new potatoes, halved
¼ cup (60g) soured cream
¼ cup (75g) mayonnaise
2 tablespoons drained green
    peppercorns, chopped coarsely
2 tablespoons french dressing

1   Combine chicken, garlic, juice, pepper and half of the basil in medium bowl; toss to coat chicken all over in marinade.

2   Cook chicken, in batches, on heated oiled grill plate or barbecue, brushing occasionally with marinade until browned and cooked through. Cover to keep warm.

3   Cook pancetta on heated oiled grill plate or barbecue about 1 minute each side or until crisp; chop coarsely.

4   Meanwhile, boil, steam or microwave potato until just tender; drain. Divide potato among serving plates; drizzle with combined soured cream, mayonnaise, peppercorns, dressing, remaining basil and pancetta. Serve chicken with hot potato salad.

preparation time 15 minutes
cooking time 20 minutes
serves 4
per serving 25.2g fat; 1822kJ (436 cal)

thyme chicken
with grilled citrus

2 tablespoons olive oil
2 teaspoons dijon mustard
2 tablespoons fresh thyme leaves
4 single chicken breast fillets (700g)
2 medium lemons (280g)
2 limes
¼ cup (60g) dijon mustard, extra

1 Combine oil, mustard and half of the thyme in medium bowl; add chicken. Cover; refrigerate 3 hours or overnight. Drain chicken; reserve marinade.
2 Cook chicken on heated oiled barbecue, uncovered, until browned both sides and cooked through, brushing occasionally with reserved marinade during cooking.
3 Meanwhile, cut each lemon into six wedges and each lime into four wedges; cook on heated oiled barbecue until browned all over.
4 Combine remaining mustard and thyme in small bowl. Serve chicken with citrus wedges and mustard.

preparation time 15 minutes
(plus marinating time)
cooking time 15 minutes
serves 4
per serving 19.4g fat; 1470kJ
(351 cal)

balsamic-seared steak with potatoes & mushrooms

¼ cup (60ml) balsamic vinegar
2 cloves garlic, crushed
4 beef scotch fillet steaks (800g)
1kg salad potatoes, quartered lengthways
1 tablespoon olive oil
500g flat mushrooms, sliced thickly
2 tablespoons dry red wine
1 tablespoon plum jam
1 tablespoon cornflour
¾ cup (180ml) beef stock

1 Combine vinegar and garlic in medium bowl, add beef; toss beef to coat in marinade. Cover; refrigerate 3 hours or overnight.
2 Preheat oven to moderately hot.
3 Place potato, in single layer, in large shallow baking dish; drizzle with oil. Roast, uncovered, in moderately hot oven, stirring occasionally, about 30 minutes or until lightly browned and crisp.
4 Meanwhile, cook steaks on heated lightly oiled barbecue or grill plate until cooked as desired. Cover to keep warm.
5 Cook mushroom on same heated barbecue or grill plate until just tender.
6 Place wine in small pan; bring to a boil. Add jam and blended cornflour and stock; stir until sauce boils and thickens slightly. Serve steaks with mushrooms, potato and sauce.

preparation time 15 minutes (plus marinating time)
cooking time 15 minutes
serves 4
per serving 13.7g fat; 2165kJ (518 cal)

There are a few simple tricks to perfectly barbecued steak – turn it once only, don't pierce it (or all the juices will escape) and let it rest afterwards. But of course there's also succulent pork spare ribs, lamb cutlets, juicy hamburgers and hot, meaty sausages…

mustard t-bone & baked potato

8 medium potatoes (1.6kg)
8 beef T-bone steaks (2kg)
⅓ cup (95g) dijon mustard
⅓ cup coarsely chopped fresh flat-leaf parsley
¼ cup coarsely chopped fresh rosemary

1 Wrap potatoes individually in foil; place in disposable baking dish. Cook in covered barbecue, using indirect heat, following manufacturer's instructions, about 1 hour or until tender.
2 Brush beef all over with mustard; cook on heated oiled barbecue, uncovered, until browned and cooked as desired. Sprinkle with combined herbs.
3 Serve beef with potato.

preparation time 10 minutes
cooking time 1 hour 10 minutes
serves 8
per serving 8.7g fat; 1456kJ (348 cal)

piquant grilled t-bone steaks

¼ cup (60ml) soy sauce
2 tablespoons oyster sauce
1 tablespoon hoisin sauce
1 tablespoon brown sugar
1 tablespoon dry sherry
1 clove garlic, crushed
1 teaspoon sesame oil
4 beef T-bone steaks (1kg)

1 Combine sauces, sugar, sherry, garlic and oil in large shallow dish; add beef. Cover; refrigerate 3 hours or overnight. Drain beef; reserve marinade.
2 Cook beef on heated oiled barbecue, uncovered, until browned and cooked as desired, brushing with reserved marinade during cooking. Serve with salad.

preparation time 5 minutes (plus marinating time)
cooking time 10 minutes
serves 4
per serving 15g fat; 1288kJ (308 cal)

fillet steaks with caramelised onion & garlic mushrooms

6 beef scotch fillet steaks (1.25kg)
½ cup (125ml) dry red wine
2 tablespoons chopped fresh basil
2 cloves garlic, crushed
20g butter
6 medium red onions (1kg), sliced thinly
⅓ cup (75g) firmly packed brown sugar
¼ cup (60ml) red wine vinegar
6 large flat mushrooms (840g)
2 tablespoons olive oil
1 clove garlic, crushed, extra
1 teaspoon lemon pepper

1 Combine beef, wine, basil and garlic in large bowl. Cover; refrigerate 3 hours or overnight.
2 Melt butter in large frying pan; cook onion, stirring, until soft and browned lightly. Stir in sugar and vinegar; cook, stirring constantly, about 20 minutes or until onion is well browned and mixture thickened.
3 Brush mushrooms with combined oil, extra garlic and lemon pepper; cook on heated oiled grill plate or barbecue until tender.
4 Drain beef; discard marinade. Cook beef, in batches, on heated oiled grill plate or barbecue until browned and cooked as desired.
5 Top each steak with a mushroom and a little caramelised onion.

preparation time 15 minutes (plus marinating time)
cooking time 35 minutes
serves 6
per serving 21.9g fat; 2069kJ (495 cal)

chilli t-bone steak with hash browns

4 beef T-bone steaks (1.2kg)
⅓ cup (80ml) worcestershire sauce
⅓ cup (80ml) hot chilli sauce
3 medium potatoes (600g)
40g butter
1 small brown onion (80g),
    chopped finely

1 Combine steaks and sauces in large bowl; toss to coat steaks all over in marinade.

2 Meanwhile, grate peeled potatoes coarsely. Using hands, squeeze excess liquid from potato; spread onto sheets of absorbent paper, squeeze again to remove as much liquid as possible from potato.

3 Heat half of the butter in large non-stick frying pan; cook onion, stirring, until soft. Add potato; stir over heat constantly until potato begins to stick to pan. Remove from heat; cool 5 minutes. Transfer potato mixture to large bowl.

4 Using wet hands, shape potato mixture into eight patties. Heat remaining butter in same pan; cook hash browns, in batches, until browned and crisp on both sides. Drain on absorbent paper.

5 Drain steaks; discard marinade. Cook steaks, in batches, on heated oiled barbecue or grill plate until browned both sides and cooked as desired. Serve steaks with hash browns and salad, if desired.

preparation time 15 minutes
cooking time 20 minutes
serves 4
per serving 20.3g fat; 1931kJ (462 cal)

tandoori beef with grilled limes

4 beef rib-eye steaks (600g)
1 clove garlic, crushed
¼ cup (75g) tandoori paste
4 limes, halved
½ cup (160g) mango chutney
¾ cup (210g) plain yogurt

1 Combine beef, garlic and paste in large bowl. Cover; refrigerate 3 hours or overnight.
2 Cook beef on heated oiled barbecue, uncovered, until browned and cooked as desired.
3 Meanwhile, cook lime on heated oiled barbecue plate; cook about 2 minutes or until browned.
4 Serve beef with lime, chutney and yogurt; accompany with steamed beans and saffron rice, if desired.

preparation time 10 minutes (plus marinating time)
cooking time 10 minutes
serves 4
per serving 17.1g fat; 1641kJ (392 cal)

beef fajitas

⅓ cup (80ml) barbecue sauce
1 teaspoon ground cumin
1 teaspoon ground coriander
½ teaspoon chilli powder
500g beef fillet, sliced thinly
1 small red pepper (150g),
    deseeded, sliced thinly
1 small green pepper (150g),
    deseeded, sliced thinly
1 small yellow pepper (150g),
    deseeded, sliced thinly
8 large flour tortillas
¾ cup (180g) soured cream

avocado topping
2 medium avocados (500g)
1 tablespoon lime juice
1 clove garlic, crushed

tomato salsa
2 medium tomatoes (380g),
    deseeded, chopped finely
1 small red onion (100g),
    chopped finely
1 tablespoon olive oil
2 teaspoons finely chopped
    fresh coriander

preparation time 30 minutes
(plus marinating time)
cooking time 10 minutes
serves 4
per serving 53.3g fat; 3462kJ
(827 cal)

1 Combine sauce and spices in medium bowl;
add beef. Cover; refrigerate 3 hours or overnight.
2 Cook beef and peppers on heated oiled barbecue,
uncovered, until beef is brown and peppers are tender.
3 Meanwhile, wrap tortillas in foil, in parcels of four,
and heat on barbecue. Remove tortillas from foil and
divide beef mixture among them. Top with soured
cream, avocado topping and tomato salsa; roll to
enclose filling.

avocado topping Mash avocado coarsely in
medium bowl with fork; mash in lime juice and garlic.

tomato salsa Combine ingredients in small bowl.

veal cutlets with anchovy garlic butter

1 lemon
2 cloves garlic, crushed
¼ cup (60ml) extra virgin olive oil
1 clove garlic, crushed, extra
125g butter, softened
8 small veal cutlets (1.3kg)
1 tablespoon fresh sage leaves
4 anchovy fillets, drained
1 teaspoon finely chopped fresh
   sage, extra

1 Peel rind thinly from lemon using a vegetable peeler. Cut rind into long, thin strips.
2 Combine cutlets, garlic, sage leaves, rind and oil in large bowl; toss to coat cutlets, stand 10 minutes.
3 Meanwhile, pound or chop anchovies and extra garlic together to form a paste. Beat butter in a bowl with a wooden spoon until smooth; beat in anchovy paste and extra sage until combined.
4 Cook cutlets on heated oiled barbecue or grill plate until browned on both sides and cooked as desired. Serve cutlets with anchovy butter and a mixed salad, if desired.

preparation time 15 minutes (plus marinating time)
cooking time 10 minutes
serves 4
per serving 45.6g fat; 2730kJ (653 cal)
tip The veal can be marinated, and the anchovy butter made, a day ahead.

grilled curried lamb cutlets with tomato chickpea salad

12 lamb cutlets (900g), trimmed
⅓ cup (80ml) lime juice
2 cloves garlic
1 teaspoon garam masala
2 teaspoons ground cumin
2 teaspoons ground coriander
2 limes, cut into wedges

tomato chickpea salad
2 x 300g cans chickpeas, rinsed,
    drained
2 medium tomatoes (380g), seeded,
    chopped finely
1 medium red onion (170g), chopped
    finely
1 tablespoon olive oil
2 tablespoons lemon juice
1 tablespoon coarsely chopped fresh
    coriander
1 clove garlic, crushed

1 Toss lamb in large bowl with combined juice, garlic and spices. Cover; refrigerate 3 hours or overnight.
2 Drain lamb; discard marinade.
3 Cook lamb on heated oiled barbecue, uncovered, until browned and cooked as desired.
4 Serve with lime wedges and tomato chickpea salad.

tomato chickpea salad Combine ingredients in medium bowl.

preparation time 15 minutes (plus marinating time)
cooking time 15 minutes
serves 4
per serving 17.6g fat; 1564kJ (374 cal)

pepper lamb steaks with tomato jam

2 cloves garlic, crushed
2 tablespoons cracked black pepper
2 teaspoons finely chopped fresh
   thyme
2 teaspoons finely grated lemon rind
1 tablespoon plain flour
8 lamb steaks (1.6kg)
1 tablespoon olive oil

tomato jam

3 medium tomatoes (570g), peeled,
   chopped coarsely
1 small white onion (80g), chopped
   finely
1 clove garlic, sliced thinly
1 cup (200g) firmly packed brown sugar
2 tablespoons malt vinegar
2 tablespoons lemon juice

1   Combine garlic, pepper, thyme, rind and flour in small bowl. Brush lamb with oil; press pepper mixture onto lamb. Cover; refrigerate 3 hours or overnight.
2   Cook lamb on heated oiled barbecue, uncovered, until browned and cooked as desired.
3   Serve lamb with tomato jam.

tomato jam   Combine tomato, onion and garlic in medium saucepan; bring to a boil. Boil, uncovered, about 3 minutes or until tomatoes are pulpy. Stir in sugar, vinegar and juice; boil, uncovered, about 15 minutes or until mixture becomes thick. Cool jam before serving.

preparation time 20 minutes (plus marinating time)
cooking time 35 minutes
serves 4
per serving 19.3g fat; 3070kJ (733 cal)
tip Tomato jam can be made up to a week ahead and refrigerated, covered.

lamb in fruit chutney marinade

½ cup (160g) fruit chutney
2 tablespoons olive oil
2 teaspoons french mustard
½ teaspoon cracked black pepper
4 lamb forequarter chops (760g)

1   Combine chutney, oil, mustard and pepper in large bowl; add lamb. Cover; refrigerate 3 hours or overnight.
2   Cook lamb on heated oiled barbecue, uncovered, until browned and cooked as desired.
3   Serve with saffron rice and pappadoms, if desired.

preparation time 5 minutes (plus marinating time)
cooking time 15 minutes
serves 4
per serving 17.9g fat; 1470kJ (351 cal)

sesame & honey lamb

1kg lamb eye of loin
2 cloves garlic, crushed
½ cup (175g) honey
2 teaspoons sesame oil
500g asparagus, trimmed
1 tablespoon sesame seeds, toasted

1   Combine lamb, garlic, honey and oil in large bowl. Cover; refrigerate 3 hours or overnight.
2   Drain lamb; discard marinade. Cook lamb on heated oiled barbecue until browned all over and cooked as desired. Stand 5 minutes; slice thinly.
3   Meanwhile, cook asparagus on heated oiled barbecue until tender.
4   Serve lamb with asparagus; sprinkle with seeds.

preparation time 15 minutes (plus marinating time)
cooking time 15 minutes
serves 4
per serving 13g fat; 1997kJ (477 cal)

chilli & honey lamb

2 cloves garlic, crushed
1 tablespoon wholegrain mustard
1 teaspoon grated lemon rind
2 tablespoons lemon juice
2 tablespoons honey
2 teaspoons curry powder
1 teaspoon sambal oelek
1 teaspoon ground turmeric
8 lamb cutlets (600g)

1 Combine garlic, mustard, rind, juice, honey, curry powder, sambal oelek and turmeric in medium bowl.
2 Rub mixture onto lamb; place in large bowl. Cover; refrigerate 3 hours or overnight.
3 Cook lamb on heated oiled barbecue, uncovered, until browned and cooked as desired.
4 Serve with char-grilled asparagus, red pepper and lemon, if desired.

preparation time 10 minutes (plus marinating time)
cooking time 15 minutes
serves 4
per serving 7.3g fat; 781kJ (187 cal)

greek lamb
with lemon & potatoes

2kg leg of lamb
3 cloves garlic, quartered
6 sprigs fresh oregano, halved
1 large lemon (180g)
1kg old potatoes, peeled, quartered
    lengthways
1 teaspoon finely chopped fresh thyme

1   Make 12 small cuts in lamb with a sharp knife.
Press garlic and oregano into cuts.
2   Remove rind from lemon; cut rind into long thin
strips (or remove rind with a zester). Squeeze juice
from lemon – you will need ⅓ cup of juice.
3   Place lamb, upside down, in heavy-based baking
dish; pour juice over lamb. Cover dish lightly with
foil; cook in covered barbecue, using indirect heat,
following manufacturer's instructions, 2 hours. Turn
lamb over; brush all over with pan juices.
4   Add potato to dish; sprinkle with thyme and lemon
rind. Bake, covered, further 1 hour 45 minutes.
5   Remove foil; cook, uncovered, 15 minutes or until
browned. Stand lamb, loosely covered, 10 minutes
before serving.

preparation time 20 minutes
(plus standing time)
cooking time 4 hours
serves 8
per serving 11.3g fat; 1408kJ
(336 cal)
tip This recipe produces well-
cooked but very moist, tender
meat which literally falls off the
bone. This may make it difficult
to carve, in which case simply cut
into chunks, or fork apart.

tandoori lamb cutlets with cucumber salad

¾ cup (210g) plain yogurt
2 cloves garlic, quartered
1 large brown onion (200g), chopped coarsely
2 tablespoons grated fresh ginger
¼ cup (60ml) lemon juice
1 teaspoon chilli powder
2 teaspoons garam masala
1 tablespoon sweet paprika
2 teaspoons ground cumin
12 lamb cutlets (900g), trimmed

cucumber salad

1 cucumber (260g)
2 fresh red thai chillies, deseeded, chopped finely
¼ cup (60ml) groundnut oil
1½ tablespoons lemon juice
1 clove garlic, crushed
2 teaspoons cumin seeds, toasted
1 tablespoon finely shredded fresh mint

coriander yogurt

½ cup loosely packed coriander leaves
¾ cup (210g) plain yogurt

preparation time 25 minutes (plus marinating time)
cooking time 15 minutes
serves 4
per serving 28.3g fat; 1817kJ (434 cal)
tip The tandoori marinade can also be used with poultry and seafood. It can be made up to 2 days ahead and refrigerated, covered.

1 Blend or process yogurt, garlic, onion, ginger, juice and spices until pureed.
2 Pour marinade over lamb in large bowl; stir to coat well. Cover; refrigerate 3 hours or overnight.
3 Cook undrained lamb on heated oiled barbecue, uncovered, until browned all over and cooked through.
4 Serve with cucumber salad and coriander yogurt.

cucumber salad Using a vegetable peeler, peel cucumber into long thin ribbons. Just before serving, gently toss with remaining ingredients.

coriander yogurt Blend or process coriander and yogurt until combined.

lamb chops with sun-dried tomato pesto

6 lamb chump chops (660g)
½ cup (125ml) lemon juice
½ cup (125ml) dry white wine
2 cloves garlic, crushed

sun-dried tomato pesto
1 cup (150g) drained sun-dried
    tomatoes
½ cup (125ml) olive oil
½ cup (80g) pine nuts, toasted
⅓ cup (25g) grated parmesan cheese
2 tablespoons lemon juice
2 cloves garlic, crushed

1 Trim fat from lamb. Place lamb in shallow dish; pour over combined juice, wine and garlic. Cover; refrigerate 3 hours or overnight.
2 Drain lamb; discard marinade.
3 Cook lamb on heated oiled barbecue, uncovered, until browned and cooked as desired.
4 Serve with sun-dried tomato pesto.

sun-dried tomato pesto Blend or process ingredients until combined.

preparation time 15 minutes (plus marinating time)
cooking time 15 minutes
serves 6
per serving 41g fat; 2166kJ (517 cal)

sticky pork ribs

2 tablespoons tomato paste
2 tablespoons tomato ketchup
2 tablespoons soy sauce
1 teaspoon grated lemon rind
¼ cup (60ml) lemon juice
1 tablespoon brown sugar
1 teaspoon cracked black pepper
1 teaspoon ground allspice
¼ teaspoon chilli powder
2 cloves garlic, crushed
2kg american-style pork spare ribs

1 Combine paste, sauces, rind, juice, sugar, pepper, allspice, chilli powder and garlic in large shallow dish; add pork. Cover; refrigerate 3 hours or overnight.
2 Remove ribs from marinade; reserve marinade.
3 Place ribs in disposable baking dish. Cook ribs in covered barbecue, using indirect heat, following manufacturer's instructions, about 45 minutes or until ribs are cooked through, brushing ribs occasionally with reserved marinade during cooking.

preparation time 10 minutes (plus marinating time)
cooking time 45 minutes
serves 4
per serving 30.4g fat; 1968kJ (470 cal)

pork with caramelised pineapple

1 tablespoon grated fresh ginger
½ cup (125ml) pineapple juice
½ cup (125ml) green ginger wine
⅓ cup (115g) honey
2 tablespoons vegetable oil
8 pork butterfly steaks (1kg)
½ medium pineapple (600g), halved,
   sliced thickly

1 Combine ginger, juice, wine, honey and oil in jug.
2 Trim excess fat from pork. Place pork in shallow dish; pour over ginger mixture. Cover; refrigerate 3 hours or overnight.
3 Drain pork; reserve marinade.
4 Cook pork and pineapple on heated oiled barbecue, uncovered, until pork is browned and cooked through, brushing occasionally with reserved marinade during cooking. Serve with salad, if desired.

preparation time 15 minutes (plus marinating time)
cooking time 10 minutes
serves 4
per serving 18.1g fat; 2280kJ (545 cal)

orange-glazed ham

6kg cooked leg of ham
2 small oranges (360g), halved,
    sliced thinly
whole cloves

orange glaze
½ cup (170g) orange marmalade
¾ cup (180ml) orange juice
¼ cup (50g) firmly packed brown sugar
2 teaspoons dijon mustard
2 tablespoons Cointreau

1 Make a decorative cut through ham rind about 10cm from the shank end of leg. Make a shallow cut down centre of ham from one end to the other.
2 Place ham in disposable baking dish. Cook in covered barbecue, using indirect heat, following manufacturer's instructions, about 45 minutes or until skin begins to split.
3 Remove from barbecue; cool 15 minutes. Peel skin away from ham carefully, leaving shank end intact; discard skin. Do not cut through surface of top fat, or fat will spread during cooking. Secure orange slices with cloves in decorative pattern on ham.
4 Wrap shank in foil; brush ham with orange glaze. Cook, covered, brushing occasionally with glaze, about 2 hours or until orange slices are lightly caramelised and ham is heated through.

orange glaze Mix ingredients in small saucepan; stir over low heat until marmalade melts.

preparation time 40 minutes (plus cooling time)
cooking time 2 hours 45 minutes
serves 12
per serving 28.2g fat; 2513kJ (600 cal)
tip Grand Marnier can be substituted for the Cointreau in this recipe.

hoisin pork skewers

750g pork fillet, sliced
½ cup (125ml) hoisin sauce
2 tablespoons plum sauce
2 cloves garlic, crushed

1 Combine pork, sauces and garlic in medium bowl. Cover, refrigerate 3 hours or overnight.
2 Thread pork onto 12 skewers. Cook skewers, in batches, on heated oiled barbecue or grill plate until browned and cooked through.

preparation time 10 minutes (plus marinating time)
cooking time 10 minutes
serves 4
per serving 6.3g fat; 1250kJ (299 cal)
tip You need 12 skewers for this recipe; if using bamboo skewers, soak them in water for an hour before use to prevent them from splintering or scorching.

pork with white bean puree

2 tablespoons olive oil
2 cloves garlic, quartered
1 tablespoon lemon juice
4 x 250g pork cutlets
250g cherry tomatoes
2 x 300g can butterbeans, rinsed, drained

1 Brush pork and tomatoes with half of the oil; cook pork and tomatoes on heated oiled barbecue or grill plate until pork is browned on both sides and cooked through, and tomatoes are soft.
2 Meanwhile, place beans in medium saucepan, cover with water; bring to a boil, then simmer, uncovered, until beans are heated through.
3 Drain well. Blend or process beans with remaining oil, garlic and juice until smooth.
4 Serve pork with tomatoes, white bean puree and lemon wedges, if desired.

preparation time 10 minutes
cooking time 20 minutes
serves 4
per serving 32.8g fat; 2027kJ (485 cal)
tip The white bean puree can be made a day ahead.

sausage & caramelised onion hot dogs

25g butter
2 large brown onions (400g),
    sliced thinly
1 clove garlic, crushed
1 tablespoon brown sugar
2 teaspoons balsamic vinegar
1 tablespoon beef stock
4 thin continental sausages
4 hot dog buns
⅓ cup (80ml) tomato ketchup

1   Melt butter in medium frying pan on barbecue; cook onion and garlic, stirring, until onion is soft and browned. Add sugar, vinegar and stock; cook, stirring, until thick and syrupy.
2   Meanwhile, cook sausages on heated oiled barbecue until browned and cooked through.
3   Split each bun in half; fill with a sausage, caramelised onion and tomato ketchup.

preparation time 10 minutes
cooking time 20 minutes
serves 4
per serving 14g fat; 1524kJ (364 cal)

gourmet beef burgers

750g minced beef
1 cup (70g) stale breadcrumbs
2 tablespoons finely chopped
    fresh flat-leaf parsley
2 tablespoons sun-dried tomato paste
125g mozzarella cheese, sliced thinly
½ cup (150g) mayonnaise
4 bread rolls
50g mixed salad leaves
1 small red onion (100g), sliced thinly
2 tablespoons drained, sliced sun-dried
    tomatoes in oil

1 Combine beef, breadcrumbs, parsley and
1½ tablespoons of the tomato paste in large bowl.
Using hands, shape mixture into four burgers.
2 Cook burgers on heated oiled barbecue,
uncovered, until browned and cooked through.
Top burgers with cheese; cook until cheese melts.
3 Combine remaining paste and mayonnaise in
small bowl.
4 Split rolls in half. Place cut-side down onto
barbecue; cook until lightly toasted.
5 Sandwich burgers, mayonnaise mixture, salad,
onion and sliced tomatoes between bread rolls.

preparation time 15 minutes
cooking time 10 minutes
serves 4
per serving 39.2g fat; 3219kJ (769 cal)

sausages with tomato relish

1 tablespoon olive oil
1 clove garlic, crushed
1 large brown onion (200g),
  chopped finely
4 large tomatoes (1kg), chopped
  coarsely
2 tablespoons balsamic vinegar
3 teaspoons brown sugar
2 tablespoons torn fresh basil leaves
20 long, thin sausages

1 Heat oil in medium saucepan; cook garlic and onion, stirring, until browned lightly. Add tomato, vinegar and sugar; simmer, uncovered, stirring occasionally, about 30 minutes or until mixture is reduced by half. Just before serving, add basil.
2 Meanwhile, cook sausages on heated oiled barbecue, uncovered, until browned and cooked through.
3 Serve sausages with warm tomato relish. Sprinkle with extra basil leaves, if desired.

preparation time 10 minutes
cooking time 30 minutes
serves 10
per serving 31.4g fat; 1530kJ (365 cal)
tip Tomato relish can be made 2 days ahead and refrigerated, covered; reheat just before serving.

beef sausages with onion

¼ cup (60ml) barbecue sauce
1 tablespoon worcestershire sauce
1 tablespoon tomato ketchup
1 clove garlic, crushed
8 thick beef sausages (920g)
2 medium brown onions (300g),
   sliced thinly

1 Combine sauces and garlic in small bowl.
2 Cook sausages and onion on heated oiled barbecue, uncovered, until browned all over and cooked through, brushing sausages occasionally with sauce mixture during cooking. Serve onion over sausages.

preparation time 5 minutes
cooking time 10 minutes
serves 4
per serving 58.6g fat; 2957kJ (706 cal)

potato skins

5 medium potatoes (1kg)
2 tablespoons olive oil
2 teaspoons fine sea salt
1 teaspoon seasoned pepper
2 teaspoons finely chopped fresh rosemary
¼ cup (300g) soured cream

1 Scrub potatoes well; brush with half of the oil. Cook in covered barbecue, using indirect heat, following manufacturer's instructions, about 50 minutes or until tender; cool.
2 Cut each potato into six wedges; carefully scoop out flesh, leaving skins intact (reserve potato flesh for another use).
3 Place potato skins, skin-side up, in single layer on wire rack over disposable baking dish. Brush with remaining oil; sprinkle with combined salt, pepper and rosemary.
4 Cook in covered barbecue, using indirect heat, about 30 minutes or until crisp.
5 Serve hot with sour cream.

preparation time 25 minutes
cooking time 1 hour 20 minutes (plus cooling time)
serves 4
per serving 38.3g fat; 1578kJ (377 cal)
tip Potato skins can be prepared a day ahead and refrigerated, covered.

Barbecuing turns vegetables from bland to brilliant. It concentrates flavours and, except for leafy greens, there's barely a vegetable that can't be barbecued, either alone with a lick of oil, or in one of the delicious dishes in this chapter.

chilli, tofu & vegetable kebabs

25 small fresh red thai chillies
⅔ cup (160ml) olive oil
2 teaspoons grated lemon rind
⅓ cup (80ml) lemon juice
1 tablespoon chopped fresh oregano
1 tablespoon chopped fresh dill
2 cloves garlic, crushed
300g packet firm tofu, drained
1 large red onion (300g)
2 medium courgettes (250g)
6 medium yellow patty-pan squash
   (180g)
12 large cherry tomatoes (250g)

1   Remove and discard seeds from one of the chillies and chop finely.
2   Combine oil, rind, juice, herbs, garlic and chopped chilli in screw-top jar; shake well.
3   Cut tofu into 12 even pieces, cut onion into 12 wedges, cut courgettes into 12 pieces and cut each squash in half.
4   Thread a chilli then a piece of courgette, tofu, tomato, onion, squash and another chilli onto a skewer. Repeat with remaining skewers, chilli, tofu and vegetables.
5   Cook kebabs, in batches, on heated oiled barbecue or grill plate, brushing with half of the oil mixture, until vegetables are browned on both sides and just tender, turning only once as the tofu is delicate and breaks easily. Serve kebabs with the remaining oil mixture.

preparation time 15 minutes
cooking time 15 minutes
serves 4
per serving 42g fat; 1927kJ
(461 cal)
tips You need 12 skewers for this recipe; if using bamboo skewers, soak them in water for an hour before use to prevent them from splintering or scorching.
The chillies we used are fiery hot – warn your guests before they eat them!

char-grilled vegetables with haloumi

2 medium yellow courgettes (240g)
2 medium green courgettes (240g)
1 large red pepper (350g)
1 large yellow pepper (350g)
4 medium baby aubergines (240g)
4 spring onions (100g)
200g haloumi cheese, sliced thinly
¾ cup (180ml) olive oil
1 tablespoon caraway seeds, toasted
1 tablespoon grated lemon rind
1 clove garlic, crushed
2 teaspoons ground cumin
1 tablespoon finely chopped
    fresh lemon thyme
2 tablespoons drained, finely
    chopped capers

preparation time 30 minutes
cooking time 35 minutes
serves 6
per serving 33.8g fat; 1558kJ
(372 cal)

1 Thickly slice vegetables lengthways.
2 Cook vegetables and cheese on heated oiled barbecue, uncovered, until browned both sides and tender.
3 Transfer vegetables to large serving platter; drizzle with combined oil, seeds, rind, garlic, cumin, thyme and capers.
4 Serve vegetables topped with cheese.

courgettes with chermoulla dressing

8 medium courgettes (1kg)

chermoulla dressing
1 small red onion (100g), chopped finely
2 cloves garlic, crushed
½ teaspoon hot paprika
1 teaspoon sweet paprika
1 teaspoon ground cumin
½ cup (125ml) olive oil
2 tablespoons lemon juice
1 cup finely chopped fresh flat-leaf parsley

1 Cut courgettes in half lengthways.
2 Cook courgettes on heated oiled barbecue, uncovered, until browned lightly both sides and just tender.
3 Serve drizzled with chermoulla dressing.

chermoulla dressing Combine ingredients in screw-top jar; shake well.

preparation time 10 minutes
cooking time 10 minutes
serves 8
per serving 14.7g fat; 626kJ
tip Chermoulla, a seasoning often used as a dry marinade or rub, is an integral part of Moroccan cooking. It consists of onion, garlic, herbs and spices.

potatoes with aïoli

1kg salad potatoes

aïoli
2 egg yolks
2 tablespoons lemon juice
2 cloves garlic, crushed
¾ cup (180ml) olive oil
1 tablespoon hot water

1 Cut potatoes in half lengthways.
2 Cook potato on heated oiled barbecue until tender; serve with aïoli.

aïoli Blend or process egg yolks, juice and garlic until combined. With motor operating, gradually add oil; process until thick. Stir in the water.

preparation time 20 minutes
cooking time 20 minutes
serves 4
per serving 44.1g fat; 2346kJ (560 cal)
tip Aïoli can be made a day ahead and refrigerated, covered.

barbecued potatoes in foil

Pierce four large potatoes (1.2kg) with fork; wrap individually in foil. Cook potatoes in covered barbecue using indirect heat, following manufacturer's instructions, about 1 hour or until cooked through. Unwrap potatoes; cut a deep cross in potato. Gently squeeze with tongs to open; top with one of the following toppings.

serves 4
per serving 0.3g fat; 819kJ (196 cal)

avocado & tomato salsa

1 medium avocado (250g), chopped finely
2 medium tomatoes (380g), chopped finely
1 tablespoon coarsely chopped fresh flat-leaf parsley

1 Combine ingredients in small bowl. Serve hot potatoes topped with avocado and tomato salsa.

preparation time 15 minutes
serves 4
per serving 10g fat; 438kJ (105 cal)

sour cream & sweet chilli sauce

¾ cup (200g) soured cream
2 tablespoons sweet chilli sauce
2 tablespoons finely chopped fresh coriander

1 Combine ingredients in medium bowl; spoon onto hot potatoes.

preparation time 5 minutes
serves 4
per serving 20.1g fat; 829kJ (198 cal)

pesto butter

125g butter, softened
¼ cup (40g) pine nuts, toasted, chopped
    coarsely
¼ cup (20g) finely grated parmesan cheese
¼ cup (65g) bottled basil pesto
½ teaspoon cracked black pepper

1 Beat butter in small bowl with electric mixer
until light and creamy; stir in remaining ingredients.
Cover tightly; refrigerate until firm.
2 Serve hot potatoes topped with pesto butter.

preparation time 10 minutes (plus refrigeration
time)
cooking time 3 minutes
serves 4
per serving 40.7g fat; 1605kJ (383 cal)

bacon & cheese

3 rashers bacon (210g), sliced thinly
1 cup (125g) grated cheddar cheese
2 tablespoons finely chopped fresh chives

1 Cook bacon, stirring, in heated medium frying pan
until browned and crisp; drain on absorbent paper.
2 Sprinkle cheese over hot potatoes; top with bacon
and chives.

preparation time 10 minutes
cooking time 10 minutes
serves 4
per serving 15.2g fat; 887kJ (212 cal)

garlic celeriac

1 large celeriac (1.5kg)
1 large garlic bulb
2 tablespoons olive oil
⅓ cup chopped fresh flat-leaf parsley
⅓ cup (95g) plain yogurt

1 Peel celeriac; cut into 3cm pieces. Combine celeriac and garlic in disposable baking dish; add oil.
2 Cook in covered barbecue, using indirect heat, following manufacturer's instructions, about 1 hour or until celeriac is golden brown and tender, turning occasionally during cooking.
3 Cut garlic in half crossways; squeeze pulp over celeriac. Toss together with parsley.
4 Serve topped with yogurt.

preparation time 15 minutes
cooking time 1 hour
serves 4
per serving 10.8g fat; 809kJ (193 cal)

◀ *garlic celeriac*

pumpkin with walnut dressing

800g pumpkin, sliced thickly

walnut dressing
½ cup (50g) toasted chopped walnuts
¼ cup (60ml) lemon juice
½ cup (125ml) olive oil
1 tablespoon dijon mustard
2 tablespoons finely chopped fresh
   chives

1 Cook pumpkin on heated oiled barbecue until browned all over and tender.
2 Serve pumpkin drizzled with walnut dressing.

walnut dressing Combine ingredients in screw-top jar; shake well.

preparation time 10 minutes
cooking time 15 minutes
serves 4
per serving 37.9g fat; 1695kJ (405 cal)

potatoes & mushrooms with olives

⅓ cup (80ml) olive oil
6 unpeeled cloves garlic
5 medium potatoes (1kg), unpeeled,
    quartered
6 baby onions (150g)
350g button mushrooms
1 tablespoon fresh rosemary leaves
½ cup (60g) pitted black olives
½ cup (55g) drained sun-dried
    tomatoes in oil, halved
1 tablespoon coarsely chopped
    fresh flat-leaf parsley

1 Combine oil, garlic, potato, onions, mushrooms and rosemary in oiled disposable baking dish. Cook in covered barbecue, using indirect heat, following manufacturer's instructions, about 45 minutes or until potatoes are browned and tender, stirring occasionally during cooking.
2 Add olives and tomato; mix well. Sprinkle with parsley.

preparation time 10 minutes
cooking time 45 minutes
serves 6
per serving 13.4g fat; 1140kJ (272 cal)

lemon & garlic corn cobs

6 trimmed corn cobs (1.5kg)
2 teaspoons shredded lemon rind
1 tablespoon wholegrain mustard
2 cloves garlic, crushed
2 tablespoons coarsely chopped chives
⅓ cup (80ml) lemon juice
⅓ cup (80ml) groundnut oil

1 Cook corn on heated oiled barbecue, uncovered, until browned all over.
2 Serve corn drizzled with combined remaining ingredients.

preparation time 15 minutes
cooking time 15 minutes
serves 6
per serving 15.1g fat; 1427kJ (341 cal)
tip Recipe can be prepared 2 days ahead and refrigerated, covered.

sauces

garlic & hoisin

1 whole bulb garlic
½ cup (125ml) hoisin sauce
2 tablespoons sweet chilli sauce
1 tablespoon soy sauce
1 tablespoon rice vinegar
1 teaspoon sesame oil
2 tablespoons coarsely chopped fresh coriander

1   Place garlic on a disposable baking tray; cook in covered barbecue, using indirect heat, following manufacturer's instructions, about 45 minutes or until cloves are tender. When cool enough to handle, cut crossways in half; squeeze out garlic.
2   Combine garlic in medium bowl with sauces, vinegar and oil; whisk until smooth. Stir in coriander.

preparation time 10 minutes
cooking time 45 minutes (plus cooling time)
makes 1 cup
per tablespoon 1.2g fat; 147kJ (35 cal)
tip This Asian-style sauce goes well with pork, beef, lamb or chicken, and is good brushed over kebabs.

creamy avocado

1 large avocado (320g)
¼ cup (60g) soured cream
¼ cup (75g) mayonnaise
2 tablespoons olive oil
1 teaspoon Tabasco sauce
1 clove garlic, quartered
¼ cup tightly packed fresh coriander leaves
1 tablespoon lemon juice

1   Blend or process ingredients until smooth.

preparation time 10 minutes
makes 1½ cups
per tablespoon 7.5g fat; 303kJ (72 cal)

red onion & balsamic jam

¼ cup (60ml) olive oil
3 medium red onions (510g), sliced thinly
¼ cup (50g) firmly packed brown sugar
⅓ cup (80ml) balsamic vinegar
½ teaspoon dill seeds
¼ cup (60ml) chicken stock

1 Heat oil in medium saucepan; cook onion, stirring until soft and browned lightly.
2 Stir in sugar, vinegar, seeds and stock. Simmer, uncovered, about 20 minutes or until mixture thickens.

preparation time 10 minutes
cooking time 20 minutes
makes 1½ cups
per tablespoon 3.1g fat; 198kJ (47 cal)
tip This jam is suitable to serve with lamb and chicken.

chilli & coriander

2 large tomatoes (500g), chopped coarsely
¼ cup (60ml) water
⅓ cup (80ml) lime juice
¼ cup (50g) firmly packed brown sugar
1 teaspoon fish sauce
⅓ cup (80ml) sweet chilli sauce
2 tablespoons coarsely chopped fresh coriander

1 Combine tomato, the water, juice, sugar and sauces in medium pan; stir over low heat until sugar dissolves. Bring to a boil; reduce heat. Simmer, uncovered, about 10 minutes or until sauce thickens.
2 Remove from heat; cool. Stir in coriander.

preparation time 5 minutes
cooking time 15 minutes (plus cooling time)
makes 1 cup
per tablespoon 0.3g fat; 127kJ (30 cal)

know your salads

leafy greens

ROCKET

RADICCHIO

GREEN CORAL LETTUCE

MIXED SALAD LEAVES

RED MIGNONETTE

BABY SPINACH

RED OAK LEAF LETTUCE

GREEN OAK LEAF LETTUCE

COS LETTUCE

RED CORAL LETTUCE

CURLY ENDIVE

SWISS CHARD

ICEBERG LETTUCE

BUTTER LETTUCE

WHITE AND RED BELGIAN ENDIVE

BABY
COS LETTUCE

LAMB'S LETTUCE
(OR MÂCHE OR
CORN SALAD)

MIZUNA

77

WATERCRESS

sprouts & cresses

asian greens

MUSTARD SPROUTS
(OR MUSTARD CRESS)

PAK CHOY

MANGETOUT SPROUTS

MANGETOUT TENDRILS

WATER SPINACH
(OR KANGKUNG)

MUNG BEAN SPROUTS

ALFALFA SPROUTS

CHINESE BROCCOLI
(OR GAI LARN)

tomatoes & mushrooms

PLUM
TOMATOES

SHIITAKE
MUSHROOMS

CHERRY TOMATOES

CREMINI (OR SWISS BROWN)
MUSHROOMS

BABY PAK CHOY

T SOI
R ROSETTE
K CHOY)

GREEN
TOMATOES

FLAT (OR FIELD) MUSHROOMS

CHOY SUM
OR FLOWERING
CABBAGE)

VINE-RIPENED TOMATOES

BUTTON MUSHROOMS

caesar salad

7 slices thick white bread
2 tablespoons light olive oil
100g parmesan cheese
1 large cos lettuce
5 whole canned anchovy fillets, drained,
    halved lengthways

caesar dressing
1 egg
1 clove garlic, crushed
2 tablespoons lemon juice
½ teaspoon dijon mustard
5 whole canned anchovy fillets, drained
¾ cup (180ml) light olive oil

1 Discard crusts; cut bread into 1cm cubes.
Heat the oil in large pan; cook bread, stirring,
until browned and crisp. Drain croutons on
absorbent paper.
2 Using vegetable peeler, shave cheese into
long thin pieces.
3 Combine torn lettuce leaves with half of the
croutons, half the anchovies and half the
cheese in large bowl; add half of the dressing,
mix well. Sprinkle remaining croutons,
anchovies and cheese over salad; drizzle with
remaining dressing.

caesar dressing Blend or process egg, garlic,
juice, mustard and anchovies until smooth;
with motor operating, add oil in thin stream,
process until dressing thickens.

preparation time 25 minutes
cooking time 5 minutes
serves 4
per serving 65.1g fat; 3335kJ (797 cal)
tips Caesar salad can be served as a light
meal on its own or, as you see in many
restaurants, with pieces of grilled chicken
breast tossed in with the dressing.
The caesar dressing can be made a day ahead.
Cover and refrigerate until needed.

No barbie is complete without a favourite salad – tabbouleh, coleslaw, potato or pasta. Or try barbecuing asparagus, spring onions, mushrooms or pepper on an oiled hot plate then adding them to a green salad.

waldorf salad

4 medium (600g) red delicious apples
¼ cup (60ml) lemon juice
5 trimmed (375g) celery sticks
1 cup (120g) coarsely chopped walnuts

mayonnaise
2 egg yolks
2 teaspoons lemon juice
1 teaspoon dijon mustard
¾ cup (180ml) olive oil
1 tablespoon warm water

1 Core and coarsely chop unpeeled apples. Combine apple in small bowl with juice.
2 Coarsely chop celery.
3 Combine apple, celery and walnuts in large serving bowl with mayonnaise. Serve salad in lettuce leaves, if desired.

mayonnaise Blend or process egg yolks, juice and mustard until smooth; with motor operating, add oil in thin stream, process until mayonnaise thickens. Stir in the water.

preparation time 15 minutes
serves 4
per serving 63g fat; 2776kJ (663 cal)
tips Use warm water if the mayonnaise needs to be thinned, as it will blend into the mixture more easily. Mayonnaise can be made a day ahead and kept, covered, under refrigeration until needed.

cobb salad

½ cup (125ml) dry white wine
3 cups (750ml) water
1 tablespoon finely chopped fresh
  thyme leaves
700g chicken breast fillets
6 bacon rashers, chopped coarsely
4 hard-boiled eggs
1 small red oak leaf lettuce
100g watercress, trimmed
2 medium (500g) avocados, chopped
  coarsely
4 medium (760g) tomatoes, peeled,
  deseeded, chopped coarsely
200g blue cheese

garlic vinaigrette
¼ cup (60ml) white wine vinegar
2 tablespoons light olive oil
1 teaspoon dijon mustard
1 clove garlic, crushed

1 Combine wine, the water and thyme in large pan with chicken; bring to boil. Simmer, covered, about 20 minutes or until chicken is cooked through. Drain chicken; reserve poaching liquid for another use, if desired. When chicken is cool enough to handle, chop coarsely.
2 Meanwhile, cook bacon, stirring, in heated pan until browned and crisp; drain on absorbent paper.
3 Shell eggs, separate yolks and whites; chop egg whites coarsely, push yolks through fine sieve.
4 Divide lettuce and watercress among serving plates, top with chicken, bacon, egg white, egg yolk, avocado, tomato and crumbled cheese; drizzle salad with vinaigrette.

garlic vinaigrette Combine ingredients in screw-top jar; shake well.

preparation time 30 minutes (plus cooling time)
cooking time 20 minutes serves 4
per serving 70.7g fat; 4076kJ (974 cal)
tip Leftover roast turkey, minus the skin and bones, can be substituted for the chicken.

83

gado gado

Gado gado translates roughly as 'mixed mixed' which helps explain the casual way Indonesians eat this salad. Each diner makes his or her personal selection from the assortment of vegetables then mixes them together, dollops on the peanut sauce and mixes the salad again. Gado gado can be eaten at room temperature or cold.

2 medium (400g) potatoes, sliced
   thickly
2 medium (240g) carrots, sliced thickly
150g green beans, chopped
½ small (600g) green cabbage
vegetable oil, for deep-frying
300g firm tofu, cut into 2cm cubes
2 medium (380g) tomatoes, cut into
   wedges
1 (260g) cucumber, sliced thickly
2 cups (160g) beansprouts
4 hard-boiled eggs, quartered

peanut sauce
1 cup (150g) roasted unsalted peanuts
1 tablespoon groundnut oil
1 small (80g) brown onion, chopped
   finely
1 clove garlic, crushed
3 red thai chillies, deseeded,
   chopped finely
1 tablespoon finely grated fresh
   galangal
1 tablespoon lime juice
1 tablespoon brown sugar
½ teaspoon shrimp paste
1 cup (250ml) coconut milk
¼ teaspoon thick tamarind concentrate
1 tablespoon ketjap manis

1 Boil, steam or microwave potato, carrot and beans, separately, until potato is cooked through and carrot and beans are just tender.
2 Meanwhile, drop cabbage leaves into large pan of boiling water; remove leaves and quickly plunge into cold water. Drain cabbage; slice finely.
3 Heat oil in small pan; deep-fry tofu, in batches, until browned. Drain on absorbent paper.
4 Place potato, carrot, beans, cabbage, tofu, tomato, cucumber, beansprouts and egg in sections on serving plate; serve with peanut sauce.
5 Serve as a vegetarian snack or with rice and chicken, fish, shellfish, lamb or beef.

peanut sauce Process nuts until chopped coarsely. Heat the oil in small pan; cook onion, garlic and chilli, stirring, until onion is golden brown. Add peanuts and remaining ingredients; bring to boil. Simmer 5 minutes or until mixture thickens; cool 10 minutes. Pour sauce into small bowl and serve to accompany the vegetable salad.

preparation time 1 hour
cooking time 35 minutes
serves 4
per serving 47g fat; 2990kJ (714 cal) (excludes oil for deep-frying)
tip Substitute fresh ginger for the galangal if it is not available.

beetroot salad

4 medium (700g) fresh beetroot
3 medium (600g) salad potatoes
1 cup (180g) shelled fresh peas
1 small (100g) red onion, chopped finely

sour cream dressing
1 egg yolk
2 teaspoons dijon mustard
2 teaspoons white vinegar
½ cup (125ml) olive oil
½ cup (125ml) soured cream

1 Trim beetroot, leaving about 1cm at both stem and root ends; avoid piercing the beetroot as colour will leach. Wrap trimmed beetroot, separately, in foil; bake in hot oven 40 minutes or until tender. Cool 10 minutes; peel, cut into wedges.
2 Meanwhile, peel potatoes; cut into wedges. Boil, steam or microwave potato and peas, separately, until just tender; drain.
3 Place beetroot, potato, peas, onion and sour cream dressing in large bowl; toss gently to combine. Serve warm or chilled.

sour cream dressing Blend or process egg yolk, mustard and vinegar until smooth. With motor operating, add oil in thin stream; process until dressing thickens. Transfer dressing to small bowl, stir in sour cream.

preparation time 20 minutes
cooking time 40 minutes
serves 4
per serving 43.9g fat; 2324kJ (555 cal)

tips Potatoes and beetroot can be cooked a day ahead; cover and refrigerate until ready to make salad. We used fresh beetroot and peas in this recipe, but you can use canned whole baby beetroot and frozen peas, if desired.
You will need approximately 450g fresh peas-in-the-pod to give 180g of shelled peas.
To lower the fat count, use the reduced-fat, instead of the full-fat, version of soured cream.

salade niçoise

1 medium (170g) red onion
4 medium (300g) plum tomatoes
3 trimmed (225g) celery stalks
3 hard-boiled eggs
200g green beans
12 whole canned anchovy fillets,
    drained, halved lengthways
425g can tuna in oil, drained, flaked
100g niçoise olives
2 tablespoons baby capers
2 tablespoons shredded basil leaves

lemon garlic dressing
½ cup (125ml) extra virgin olive oil
¼ cup (60ml) lemon juice
1 clove garlic, crushed
1 teaspoon sugar

1   Quarter onion lengthways; slice thinly. Cut tomatoes into wedges; remove seeds. Slice celery thinly. Shell and quarter eggs.
2   Top and tail beans; boil, steam or microwave beans until just tender, drain. Rinse beans under cold water; drain well.
3   Layer onion, tomato, celery, egg, beans, anchovy and tuna on serving plate. Sprinkle with olives, capers and basil; drizzle with lemon garlic dressing.

lemon garlic dressing   Combine all ingredients in screw-top jar; shake well.

preparation time 1 hour
cooking time 5 minutes
serves 4
per serving 50.3g fat; 2646kJ (632 cal)
tip Niçoise olives, tiny ovate brown-black olives with a rich nutty flavour, are grown all over the rough, hilly terrain of Provence. You'll find them in some supermarkets and delicatessens.
If unavailable, substitute any small brown olive.

greek salad

4 medium (300g) plum tomatoes
1 (260g) cucumber
2 medium (400g) green peppers
1 medium (170g) red onion
1 cup (160g) kalamata olives, pitted
150g Greek sheep's milk feta cheese
1 teaspoon crushed dried rigani
½ cup (125ml) extra virgin olive oil

1 Quarter tomatoes and cucumber lengthways; cut into chunks. Slice pepper into rings; remove and discard seeds and membranes. Cut onion into wedges.

2 Combine tomato, cucumber, pepper, onion and olives in large serving bowl.

3 Break cheese into large pieces and place on top of salad, sprinkle with rigani; drizzle with oil.

preparation time 25 minutes
serves 4
per serving 39.6g fat; 1779kJ (425 cal)
tips For an authentic Greek way of presenting this salad, leave the feta in a whole piece and sit it on the top of the salad. Anchovies can be added to impart a salty flavour.

Rigani is a type of oregano which grows wild in the mountains of Greece and tastes rather sharper than strong oregano; if you can't find it in your area, substitute a mixture of fresh or dried oregano and/or marjoram. Adjust the amount used to suit your taste.

chef's salad

350g chicken breast fillets
3 medium (225g) plum tomatoes
1 large cos lettuce
200g finely sliced leg ham
100g finely sliced Jarlsberg cheese
3 hard-boiled eggs, quartered

vinaigrette
½ cup (125ml) olive oil
¼ cup (60ml) white wine vinegar
2 teaspoons wholegrain mustard
1 teaspoon sugar
¼ teaspoon cracked white pepper

1 Cook chicken in heated oiled large pan until browned both sides. Place in shallow baking dish; bake, uncovered, in moderate oven about 15 minutes or until cooked through. Cool 5 minutes; slice thinly.
2 Cut each tomato into 8 wedges. Wash and separate lettuce leaves; tear into small pieces.
3 Divide lettuce among serving bowls; layer with chicken, tomato, ham, cheese and egg, then drizzle with vinaigrette.

vinaigrette Combine ingredients in screw-top jar; shake well.

preparation time 20 minutes (plus cooling time)
cooking time 25 minutes
serves 4
per serving 48.2g fat; 2737kJ (654 cal)
tips Gruyère or Emmenthal can be used in place of the Jarlsberg cheese, and prosciutto substitutes wonderfully for the leg ham.
You can prepare the vinaigrette a day ahead; keep it, covered, in the refrigerator.

grilled vegetable salad

2 medium (400g) green peppers
2 medium (400g) red peppers
2 medium (400g) yellow peppers
1 large (300g) red onion
2 medium (240g) green courgettes
2 medium (240g) yellow courgettes
6 baby (360g) aubergines

balsamic dressing
2 tablespoons lemon juice
1 clove garlic, crushed
¼ cup (60ml) olive oil
2 tablespoons balsamic vinegar
1 tablespoon chopped fresh oregano

1 Quarter peppers, discard seeds and membranes. Cut into thick strips. Cut onion into 8 wedges. Cut courgettes and aubergines lengthways into thin slices.
3 Cook vegetables, in batches, in heated oiled grill pan (or on grill or barbecue) until browned all over and tender. Combine all vegetables in large bowl; drizzle with balsamic dressing, mix well.

balsamic dressing Combine all ingredients in screw-top jar; shake well.

preparation time 15 minutes
cooking time 20 minutes
serves 6
per serving 10.2g fat; 637kJ (152 cal)
tip Make this salad a day in advance, to let the grilled vegetables infuse with the flavour of the dressing.

▼ *rocket & parmesan salad*

rocket & parmesan salad

60g parmesan cheese
200g baby rocket leaves
80g semi-dried tomatoes, halved lengthways
¼ cup (40g) pine nuts, toasted
¼ cup (60ml) balsamic vinegar
¼ cup (60ml) extra virgin olive oil

1 Using vegetable peeler, shave cheese into wide, long pieces.
2 Combine rocket with tomato and nuts in large bowl; add cheese, drizzle with combined vinegar and oil, toss gently.

preparation time 25 minutes
cooking time 3 minutes
serves 8
per serving 16g fat; 744kJ (178 cal)
tips Baby spinach can be substituted for rocket.

panzanella

1 long loaf stale ciabatta
6 medium (1.1kg) tomatoes
2 trimmed (150g) celery sticks
½ (130g) cucumber
1 medium (170g) red onion
¼ cup (60ml) red wine vinegar
½ cup (125ml) olive oil
1 clove garlic, crushed
¼ cup finely shredded fresh
   basil leaves

1 Cut ciabatta in half horizontally; reserve one half for another use. Remove and discard soft centre from remaining half; cut remaining bread into 2cm cubes.
2 Cut tomatoes into wedges; discard seeds, chop coarsely. Cut celery into 4 strips lengthways; coarsely chop strips.
3 Peel cucumber; cut in half lengthways. Cut halves into 1cm-thick slices.
4 Chop onion coarsely, combine with bread cubes, tomato, celery and cucumber in large bowl.
5 Combine remaining ingredients for dressing in screw-top jar; shake well. Pour dressing over salad; toss gently.

preparation time 25 minutes
serves 4
per serving 30.1g fat; 1600kJ (382 cal)
tips Add capers for extra flavour.
Instead of discarding the soft white centre of the bread, you can blend or process it into fine breadcrumbs, or try cutting it into small cubes and toasting until golden brown and crunchy.
For this recipe, we used ciabatta, a wood-fired white loaf readily available from most supermarkets, but any Italian crusty bread may be used in its place.

spinach, bacon & crouton salad

1 small French bread stick
1 clove garlic, crushed
¼ cup (60ml) olive oil
10 (320g) extra thin bacon rashers
1 egg yolk
2 teaspoons dijon mustard
¼ teaspoon tabasco sauce
1 tablespoon white vinegar
2 teaspoons lemon juice
2 tablespoons cream
1 clove garlic, crushed, extra
½ cup (125ml) extra virgin olive oil
400g baby spinach leaves
5 hard-boiled eggs

preparation time 25 minutes
cooking time 20 minutes
serves 6
per serving 30.3g fat; 1613kJ (385 cal)
tips To keep spinach crisp, pick the freshest leaves and rinse under cold water. Shake, then place in an airtight plastic bag and refrigerate for several hours or overnight.
We used extra thin bacon rashers; you can substitute prosciutto if you wish.

1 Cut bread in half lengthways, cut halves into 5mm slices; place in single layer on oven tray. Brush bread slices on one side with combined garlic and olive oil; toast in moderate oven about 8 minutes or until croutons are browned lightly.

2 Remove rind and trim fat from bacon; cut rashers into quarters. Cook in heated oiled pan until crisp; drain on kitchen paper. When bacon is cold, crumble.

3 Combine yolk, mustard, sauce, vinegar, juice, cream and extra garlic in small bowl. Gradually whisk in the extra virgin olive oil. Gently toss spinach and dressing in large serving bowl.

4 Shell hard-boiled eggs; chop coarsely. Add eggs, croutons and bacon to bowl; toss gently to combine.

shredded, grated great slaws

*A new take on an old favourite can make a welcome change at mealtimes.
So three delicious versions of coleslaw, with a range of ingredients that lend
an international flavour, will have you tucking into your meal with renewed gusto.*

crunchy fried noodle coleslaw

10 trimmed (150g) radishes
1 large (350g) red pepper, sliced thinly
1 small (450g) Chinese cabbage, shredded
6 spring onions, chopped finely
1 cup (80g) beansprouts
½ cup (70g) slivered almonds, toasted
2 x 100g packets fried noodles

sweet-sour dressing
⅔ cup (160ml) groundnut oil
2 tablespoons white wine vinegar
2 tablespoons brown sugar
2 tablespoons soy sauce
2 teaspoons sesame oil
1 clove garlic, crushed

1 Slice radishes into matchstick-size
pieces.
2 Combine radish in large bowl with
pepper, cabbage, onion, beansprouts,
nuts and noodles.
3 Pour sweet-sour dressing over salad;
toss to combine.

sweet-sour dressing Combine all
ingredients in screw-top jar; shake well.

preparation time 35 minutes
serves 8
per serving 37.1g fat; 1914kJ (457 cal)
tip For extra heat, try adding
1 tablespoon Thai sweet chilli sauce or
1 finely chopped chilli to the dressing.

red cabbage, apple & caraway coleslaw

2 medium (300g) green apples
½ medium (800g) red cabbage, shredded finely
2 tablespoons caraway seeds, toasted
2 teaspoons dijon mustard
½ cup (125ml) olive oil
2 tablespoons raspberry vinegar

1 Core unpeeled apples; cut into matchstick-size pieces.
2 Combine apple pieces in large bowl with cabbage and caraway seeds; drizzle with combined remaining ingredients, toss to combine.

oreparation time 15 minutes
serves 8
per serving 15.6g fat; 738kJ (176 cal)
tip If your supermarket doesn't stock raspberry vinegar, use any fruit-flavoured vinegar in this recipe.
This salad, German in origin, can be served either warm or cold.

pamela's coleslaw

1 medium (1.5kg) white cabbage, shredded finely
15 spring onions, chopped finely
2 red thai chillies, deseeded, chopped finely
1 cup coarsely chopped fresh mint leaves
½ cup coarsely chopped fresh flat-leaf parsley
¼ cup coarsely chopped fresh coriander

lemon dressing
¼ cup (60ml) lemon juice
1 tablespoon dijon mustard
½ cup (125ml) groundnut oil

1 Combine cabbage in large bowl with onion, chilli and herbs.
2 Pour over lemon dressing; toss to combine.

lemon dressing Combine all ingredients inscrew-top jar; shake well.

preparation time 20 minutes
serves 8
per serving 15.2g fat; 747kJ (178 cal)
tip Use rubber gloves when deseeding and chopping chillies, as they can burn your skin.

pasta salad

375g pasta shells
6 bacon rashers
1½ cups (375ml) mayonnaise
⅓ cup (90g) wholegrain mustard
¾ cup (180ml) buttermilk
3 trimmed (225g) celery stalks,
  sliced thinly
1 large (350g) red pepper,
  chopped finely
1 bunch (15g) fresh chives,
  chopped finely
2 tablespoons finely chopped
  fresh flat-leaf parsley

1 Cook pasta in large pan of boiling water, uncovered, until just tender. Cool.
2 Meanwhile, remove and discard rind from bacon then cut into small pieces. Cook bacon, stirring, in heated medium pan until brown and crisp; drain on absorbent paper.
3 Whisk mayonnaise, mustard and buttermilk in large bowl. Add pasta, bacon and remaining ingredients; toss gently to combine.

preparation time 30 minutes
cooking time 15 minutes
serves 6
per serving 19.5g fat; 1736kJ (415 cal)
tips Rinse cooked, drained pasta under warm water, then under cold water, to prepare salad more quickly. Blend about 2 teaspoons of curry powder with the mayonnaise mixture for another flavour variation.

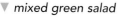

▼ *mixed green salad*

mixed green salad

250g mixed salad leaves

vinaigrette
½ cup (125ml) olive oil
½ cup (125ml) white wine vinegar
¼ cup finely chopped fresh flat-leaf parsley
2 teaspoons dijon mustard

1 Gently rinse salad leaves in cold water; dry thoroughly in salad spinner.
2 Place salad leaves in large serving bowl; add vinaigrette, toss gently.

vinaigrette Combine all ingredients in a screw-top jar or bottle with a tight-fitting stopper; shake well.

preparation time 10 minutes
serves 8
per serving 14.9g fat; 567kJ (135 cal)

tempting rice salads

Versatile rice proves how easily a deliciously different salad can be prepared in a hurry – just add your choice of ingredients to render a rice salad creamy and luscious or crunchy and supremely healthy.

white rice salad

1 (400g) corn cob
3 cups (300g) cooked white
   long-grain rice (you will need to cook
   approximately 1 cup white long-grain rice)
1 (200g) red pepper, chopped finely
1 (200g) yellow pepper, chopped finely
1 (200g) green pepper, chopped finely
2 (380g) tomatoes, deseeded, chopped finely
4 (60g) radishes, chopped finely
1 small (100g) red onion, chopped finely
1 medium (250g) avocado, chopped finely
⅓ cup (80ml) lime juice
2 tablespoons groundnut oil
¼ cup finely chopped fresh coriander

1 Remove husk and silk from corn; boil, steam or microwave until just tender, cut kernels from cob.
2 Place corn in large bowl with remaining ingredients; toss gently to combine.

preparation time 15 minutes
cooking time 5 minutes
serves 8
per serving 11g fat; 990kJ (236 cal)

brown rice salad

500g small cooked prawns
2 cups (200g) cooked brown rice (you will need
    to cook approximately ⅔ cup brown rice)
1 medium (200g) red pepper, chopped finely
3 spring onions, sliced finely
2 trimmed (150g) celery stalks, chopped finely
2 tablespoons lemon juice
2 tablespoons light olive oil
2 tablespoons cream
2 tablespoons finely chopped fresh chives
1 teaspoon sugar

1 Shell and devein prawns; chop.
2 Place prawns in large bowl with rice, pepper,
onion, celery and combined remaining ingredients;
toss gently to combine.

preparation time 15 minutes
cooking time 15 minutes
serves 8
per serving 7.5g fat; 603kJ (144 cal)

wild rice salad

1 cup (180g) uncooked wild rice
20g butter
250g button mushrooms, sliced
1 clove garlic, crushed
2 tablespoons dry red wine
3 trimmed (225g) celery sticks
1 cup (100g) pecans, halved lengthways
½ cup (85g) raisins
2 tablespoons red wine vinegar
1 teaspoon grated orange rind
¼ cup (60ml) orange juice
¼ cup light olive oil
1 teaspoon sugar

1 Cook rice in boiling water about 20 minutes or
until tender, drain.
2 Heat butter in large pan; cook mushrooms and
garlic, stirring, until browned. Add wine; cook,
stirring, about 1 minute or until wine has almost
evaporated
3 Cut celery into thin slices; place in large bowl with
rice, mushroom mixture, nuts, raisins and combined
remaining ingredients; toss gently to combine.

preparation time 15 minutes
cooking time 25 minutes
serves 8
per serving 12.4g fat; 1040kJ (248 cal)

rice & chickpea salad

1 cup (200g) white long-grain rice
2 cups (500ml) water
300g can chickpeas, rinsed, drained
¼ cup (40g) sultanas
¼ cup (35g) dried apricots, chopped
   finely
2 spring onions, sliced thinly
2 tablespoons toasted pine nuts

balsamic orange dressing
1 teaspoon finely grated orange rind
⅓ cup (80ml) orange juice
1 tablespoon balsamic vinegar
1 clove garlic, crushed
1cm piece fresh ginger (5g), grated

1 Combine rice and the water in medium heavy-based saucepan. Bring to a boil then reduce heat; simmer, covered, about 8 minutes or until rice is tender. Remove from heat; stand, covered, 10 minutes. Fluff rice with fork; cool then refrigerate, covered, until cold.
2 Meanwhile, make dressing.
3 Combine rice with remaining ingredients in large bowl; add balsamic orange dressing, toss gently to combine.

balsamic orange dressing Combine all ingredients in screw-topped jar; shake well.

preparation time 15 minutes
cooking time 10 minutes (plus standing and refrigeration time)
serves 6
per serving 4.3g fat; 929kJ (222 cal)

mozzarella & basil salad

8 medium (600g) plum tomatoes, halved
1 tablespoon olive oil
1 tablespoon balsamic vinegar
¼ teaspoon cracked black pepper
240g mozzarella cheese, sliced
¼ cup loosely packed fresh basil leaves

caper dressing
1 tablespoon capers, drained
2 tablespoons olive oil
2 tablespoons balsamic vinegar
1 clove garlic, crushed

1 Place tomato, cut-side up, on oven tray; drizzle with oil and vinegar, sprinkle with pepper. Bake tomato, uncovered, in low oven about 2 hours or until soft.
2 Alternate layers of tomato, cheese and basil onto serving plate; drizzle with caper dressing.

caper dressing Chop capers finely; combine with remaining ingredients in screw-top jar; shake well.

preparation time 15 minutes
cooking time 2 hours
serves 4
per serving 28.4g fat; 1478kJ (353 cal)

101

spicy sausage & couscous salad

500g spicy beef sausages
1½ cups (375ml) beef stock
1½ cups (300g) couscous
20g butter
1 tablespoon finely grated lemon rind
¾ cup coarsely chopped fresh flat-leaf
   parsley
120g baby rocket leaves
⅓ cup (50g) toasted pine nuts
2 fresh red thai chillies, deseeded,
   sliced thinly
1 small red onion (100g), sliced thinly
1 clove garlic, crushed
⅓ cup (80ml) lemon juice
2 tablespoons olive oil

1 Cook sausages on heated grill plate (or grill or barbecue) until browned and cooked through. Drain on absorbent paper; slice thickly.
2 Meanwhile, bring stock to a boil in medium saucepan. Remove from heat; stir in couscous and butter. Cover; stand about 10 minutes or until liquid is absorbed, fluffing couscous with fork occasionally.
3 Place sausage and couscous in large bowl with remaining ingredients; toss gently to combine.

preparation time 15 minutes
cooking time 10 minutes
serves 4
per serving 45g fat; 3621kJ (865 cal)

mixed green salad with pine nuts in lime vinaigrette

4 spring onions
400g mixed salad leaves
¼ cup (40g) pine nuts, toasted

lime vinaigrette
¼ cup (60ml) lime juice
¼ cup (60ml) groundnut oil
2 cloves garlic, crushed
1 teaspoon sugar

1 Cut onions into 10cm lengths; slice thinly lengthways. Place onion in bowl of iced water; stand about 10 minutes or until onion curls.
2 Place drained onion in large bowl with mesclun and pine nuts; toss gently with lime vinaigrette.

lime vinaigrette Combine ingredients in screw-top jar; shake well.

preparation time 15 minutes (plus standing time)
serves 8
per serving 10.5g fat; 447kJ (107 cal)

baked beetroot salad with beans, feta & mint

¼ cup (50g) dried cannellini beans
1 medium beetroot (175g), diced
cooking-oil spray
50g goat's milk feta, crumbled
50g mixed salad leaves
¼ cup loosely packed fresh mint leaves

apple dressing
2 tablespoons fresh apple juice
2 teaspoons american mustard

1 Place beans in small bowl, cover with water; stand overnight, drain. Rinse under cold water; drain.
2 Cook beans in small uncovered pan of boiling water until just tender. Rinse under cold water; drain.
3 Preheat oven to moderately hot.
4 Place beetroot in shallow baking dish; spray with oil. Bake, covered, about 20 minutes or until tender.
5 Meanwhile, make apple dressing.
6 Place beans and beetroot in bowl with remaining ingredients and dressing; toss gently to combine.

apple dressing
Place all ingredients in screw-top jar; shake well.

preparation time 10 minutes (plus standing time)
cooking time 50 minutes serves 1
per serving 10.3g fat; 1417kJ (339 cal)
tip Canned cannellini or butter beans can be used in this recipe; drain and rinse beans before using.

potato salad

7 large (2kg) salad potatoes
1 large (200g) brown onion, chopped finely
6 spring onions, chopped finely
2 tablespoons finely chopped fresh tarragon
5 hard-boiled eggs, chopped coarsely
¾ cup (180ml) mayonnaise
¾ cup (180ml) soured cream
1 tablespoon wholegrain mustard
1 clove garlic, crushed
2 tablespoons finely chopped fresh chives

1   Peel potatoes; chop into 2cm cubes.
Boil, steam or microwave potato until just
tender, drain; cool.
2   Place potato in large bowl with onions,
tarragon, egg and combined remaining
ingredients; toss gently to combine.

preparation time 25 minutes (plus cooling
time)
cooking time 20 minutes
serves 8
per serving 23g fat; 1555kJ (371 cal)
tip Keep potatoes submerged in cold water
after peeling, to avoid discolouration.

hot potato salad

4 eggs
4 bacon rashers, chopped
750g tiny new potatoes
2 pickled gherkins, chopped finely
1 tablespoon finely chopped flat-leaf parsley
⅔ cup (160ml) mayonnaise
⅓ cup (80ml) soured cream
2 teaspoons lemon juice

1   Cover eggs with water in medium pan; bring
to boil. Simmer, uncovered, 10 minutes; drain.
Cool eggs under cold water; shell and halve.
2   Meanwhile, fry bacon in dry heated pan until
browned and crisp; drain on absorbent paper.
3   Boil, steam or microwave potatoes until
tender; drain and halve.
4   Combine remaining ingredients in large
pan; stir over low heat until just hot. Combine
mayonnaise mixture with potato, bacon and
egg and toss gently.

preparation time 10 minutes
cooking time 15 minutes
serves 4
per serving 31g fat; 2106kJ (503 cal)

tabbouleh

3 medium (570g) tomatoes
½ cup (80g) bulgur wheat
5 cups tightly packed fresh flat-leaf
   parsley
1 medium (170g) red onion
1 cup tightly packed fresh mint leaves
¼ cup (60ml) lemon juice
¼ cup (60ml) extra virgin olive oil

1 Chop tomatoes finely, retaining as much of the juice as possible. Place tomato and juice on top of bulgur in small bowl, cover; refrigerate at least 2 hours or until bulgur is soft.

2 Meanwhile, cut flat-leaf parsley coarsely with scissors or chop coarsely with knife; chop onion finely, chop mint coarsely. Keep chopped ingredients separate.

3 Combine parsley, onion and mint in large bowl. Add the bulgur-tomato mixture to the bowl along with the remaining ingredients; toss gently to combine.

preparation time 40 minutes (plus refrigeration time)
serves 4
per serving 14.9g fat; 862kJ (206 cal)
tip Bulgur, often mistakenly thought to be the same as cracked wheat, is a wheat kernel that has been steamed, dried and crushed. It comes in a variety of grinds – coarse, medium and fine – and can be bought from health food stores, delicatessens and supermarkets under various names: burghul, bulghur wheat or Lebanese crushed wheat. Do not substitute with ordinary unprocessed cracked wheat.

coronation chicken

1 tablespoon olive oil
850g chicken breast fillets
½ cup (125ml) mayonnaise
½ cup (125ml) soured cream
¼ cup (90g) mango chutney
2 teaspoons curry powder
300g seedless green grapes
1 cup (100g) walnuts, chopped
    coarsely
125g mangetout sprouts

1 Heat oil in large pan; cook chicken, in batches, until browned both sides.
2 Place chicken in shallow medium baking dish; cover, bake in moderate oven about 20 minutes or until cooked through. Cool 10 minutes; cut diagonally into 5mm-wide slices.
3 Place mayonnaise, soured cream, chutney and curry powder in small bowl; whisk until smooth.
4 Remove grapes from stems.
5 Gently toss chicken with grapes, chopped walnuts and mayonnaise mixture in large bowl.
6 Serve with mangetout sprouts or a crisp green salad.

preparation time 20 minutes
cooking time 30 minutes
serves 6
per serving 33g fat; 2128kJ (508 cal)
tips The mayonnaise mixture can be made a day ahead; keep, covered, in refrigerator. Chicken is best prepared on the day of serving.
This salad will taste even better with your own homemade mayonnaise. Blend or process 2 egg yolks, 2 teaspoons lemon juice and 1 teaspoon Dijon mustard until smooth. With motor operating, add ¾ cup (180ml) light olive oil in thin stream; process until mayonnaise thickens. Thin with 1 tablespoon warm water, if necessary.

brilliant bean salads

Beyond the 4-bean mix: these fabulous bean salads quicken the pulse and shed new light on an old staple – you'll wonder how you ever lived without them.

jamaican black bean salad

2 cups (400g) dried black beans
5 medium (375g) plum tomatoes, deseeded, chopped finely
250g yellow cherry tomatoes, chopped
75g baby spinach leaves, shredded
1 medium (170g) red onion, chopped finely
4 spring onions, chopped finely

chilli dressing
1 clove garlic, quartered
⅓ cup (80ml) lime juice
½ teaspoon sugar
2 tablespoons white vinegar
⅓ cup (80ml) olive oil
2 tablespoons finely chopped fresh coriander leaves
½ teaspoon cayenne pepper

1 Cover beans with cold water in large bowl; soak overnight, drain.
2 Cook beans in large pan of boiling water, uncovered, about 45 minutes or until tender; drain, cool.
3 Place beans in large bowl with tomatoes, spinach and onions; add chilli dressing, toss gently to combine.

chilli dressing Blend or process garlic, juice, sugar, vinegar and oil until dressing thickens slightly; stir in coriander and pepper.

preparation time 20 minutes (plus soaking and cooling time)
cooking time 45 minutes
serves 8
per serving 10.6g fat; 981kJ (234 cal)
tip Dried black beans are also called turtle beans; these full-flavoured dried beans bear no resemblance to the fermented soy beans, also known as black beans, that are commonly used in Chinese cooking.

roasted tomato & cannellini bean salad

2 cups (400g) dried cannellini beans
6 large (540g) plum tomatoes, quartered
⅓ cup (80ml) olive oil
½ teaspoon cracked black pepper
1 tablespoon finely grated lemon rind
¼ cup whole fresh basil leaves
1¾ cups (210g) black olives, pitted, halved
1 clove garlic, crushed
⅓ cup (80ml) lemon juice
1 teaspoon sugar

1 Cover beans with cold water in large bowl; soak overnight, drain.
2 Cook beans in large pan of boiling water, uncovered, about 45 minutes or until tender; drain, cool.
3 Meanwhile, place tomato in large baking dish; drizzle with half of the oil, sprinkle with pepper. Bake, uncovered, in very hot oven about 30 minutes or until soft.
4 Place beans and tomato in large bowl with rind, basil, olives and remaining ingredients; toss gently to combine.

preparation time 15 minutes (plus soaking time)
cooking time 45 minutes
serves 8
per serving 12g fat; 1048kJ (250 cal)
tip We used dried cannellini beans but you can substitute four 300g cans of any type of white beans, drained and rinsed, in this recipe.

greek dried bean salad

2 cups (400g) black-eyed beans
1 large (350g) yellow pepper
8 medium (600g) plum tomatoes, deseeded, chopped coarsely
2 medium (340g) red onions, chopped finely
1½ cups (240g) kalamata olives, pitted, sliced
¾ cup coarsely chopped fresh flat-leaf parsley
½ cup (125ml) red wine vinegar
2 cloves garlic, crushed
1 cup (250ml) extra virgin olive oil

1 Cover beans with cold water in large bowl; soak overnight, drain.
2 Cook beans in large pan of boiling water, uncovered, about 45 minutes or until tender; drain, cool.
3 Meanwhile, quarter pepper, remove and discard seeds and membranes. Roast under grill or in very hot oven, skin-side up, until skin blisters and blackens. Cover pepper pieces in plastic or paper for 5 minutes, peel away skin, cut into thick strips.
4 Place beans in large bowl with pepper and remaining ingredients; toss gently to combine.

preparation time 15 minutes (plus soaking and cooling time)
cooking time 45 minutes
serves 8
per serving 31.7g fat; 1407kJ (336 cal)
tip Black-eye beans have a similar flavour to cannellini beans, and one can be substituted for the other.

italian brown rice salad

3 cups (750ml) vegetable stock
2 teaspoons olive oil
1 small brown onion (80g), chopped finely
1½ cups (300g) medium-grain brown rice
1 teaspoon finely grated lime rind
⅓ cup (45g) toasted slivered almonds
⅔ cup (100g) sun-dried tomatoes, chopped coarsely
½ cup (60g) pitted black olives, chopped coarsely
½ cup coarsely chopped fresh basil
¼ cup coarsely chopped fresh flat-leaf parsley

lime and mustard dressing
2 tablespoons lime juice
2 tablespoons white wine vinegar
2 cloves garlic, crushed
2 teaspoons dijon mustard

1 Place stock in medium saucepan. Bring to a boil then reduce heat; simmer, covered.
2 Meanwhile, heat oil in large saucepan; cook onion, stirring, until softened. Add rice and rind; stir to coat rice in onion mixture.
3 Add stock. Bring to a boil then reduce heat; simmer, covered, about 50 minutes or until rice is tender and liquid is absorbed.
4 Make lime and mustard dressing.
5 Add remaining ingredients and dressing to rice mixture in pan; toss gently to combine.
6 Serve salad warm; top with fresh flat-leaf parsley, if desired.

lime and mustard dressing Place all ingredients in a screw-top jar; shake well to combine.

preparation time 15 minutes
cooking time 1 hour
serves 4
per serving 3.5g fat; 556kJ (133 cal)

111

shredded chicken & noodle salad

500g chicken breast fillets
125g rice vermicelli
1 large carrot (180g), cut into
 matchsticks
1 medium red pepper (200g),
 sliced thinly
1 medium green pepper (200g),
 sliced thinly
½ cucumber (130g), sliced thinly
1 fresh long red chilli, sliced thinly
1 cup coarsely shredded fresh mint
¼ cup (35g) toasted unsalted peanuts,
 chopped coarsely

lime and palm sugar dressing
¼ cup (60ml) lime juice
¼ cup (65g) grated palm sugar
¼ cup (60ml) fish sauce

1 Make lime and palm sugar dressing.
2 Place chicken and half of the dressing in medium saucepan with barely enough boiling water to cover chicken; bring to a boil. Reduce heat; simmer, uncovered, about 10 minutes or until chicken is cooked through. Cool chicken in poaching liquid 10 minutes; discard liquid (or reserve for another use). Using two forks, shred chicken finely.

3 Meanwhile, place rice vermicelli in large heatproof bowl; cover with boiling water. Stand until just tender; drain. Rinse under cold water; drain.
4 Place chicken and vermicelli in large bowl with carrot, peppers, cucumber, chilli, mint and remaining dressing; toss gently to combine. Divide salad among plates; top with nuts.

lime and palm sugar dressing
Place ingredients in screw-top jar; shake well.

preparation time 25 minutes
cooking time 10 minutes
serves 4
per serving 7.8g fat; 1613kJ
(386 cal)

soba salad with seaweed, ginger & vegetables

5g wakame
50g soba noodles
½ cucumber (130g), cut into
  matchsticks
1 small carrot (70g), cut into
  matchsticks
1 tablespoon toasted sesame seeds
1 spring onion, sliced thinly
1cm piece fresh ginger (5g), grated
1 teaspoon sesame oil
2 tablespoons fresh lime juice
1 teaspoon soy sauce

1 Place wakame in small bowl, cover with cold water; stand about 10 minutes or until wakame softens, drain. Discard any hard stems; chop coarsely.
2 Meanwhile, cook soba in small saucepan of boiling water, uncovered, until just tender; drain. Rinse under cold water; drain. Chop soba coarsely.
3 Place wakame and soba in medium bowl with remaining ingredients; toss gently to combine.

preparation time 10 minutes
cooking time 5 minutes
serves 1
per serving 12.2g fat; 1367kJ (327 cal)
tip Wakame, a bright green seaweed usually sold in dried form, is used in salads, soups and seasonings. It is available from most Asian food stores.

glossary

allspice also known as pimento or jamaican pepper; available whole or ground.

artichoke hearts tender centre of the globe artichoke; purchased in brine canned or in jars.

aubergine also known as eggplant. Depending on their age, they may have to be sliced and salted to reduce their bitterness. Rinse and dry well before use.

baby also known as japanese eggplant, these are small and slender. They don't need to be salted before use.

barbecue sauce a spicy, tomato-based sauce used to marinate, baste or as an accompaniment.

beansprouts also known as bean shoots; tender new growths of assorted beans and seeds germinated for consumption as sprouts.

beans

black also known as turtle beans or black kidney beans, they are an earthy-flavoured dried bean different from the better-known Chinese black beans (which are fermented soy beans). Most used in Mexico, South- and Central-America and the Caribbean, especially in soups and stews.

butterbeans also known as lima beans, sold both dried and canned. A large beige bean having a mealy texture and mild taste.

cannellini small, dried white bean similar to other Phaseolus vulgaris (great northern, navy and haricot beans).

green sometimes called french beans.

beef

rib eye (scotch fillet) the section of eye muscle which runs through the forequarter.

T-bone steak with the bone in and fillet eye attached.

beetroot also known as beets or red beets; firm, round sweet root vegetable.

ciabatta meaning 'slipper' in Italian, the traditional shape of this popular crisp-crusted white bread.

bulghur wheat also known as burghul; hulled steamed wheat kernels that, once dried, are crushed into various size grains.

butter you can use salted or unsalted butter; 125g is equal to one stick of butter.

buttermilk fresh low-fat milk cultured to give a slightly sour, tangy taste; low-fat yogurt or milk can be substituted.

capers the grey-green buds of a warm climate shrub sold either dried and salted or pickled in vinegar brine.

caraway seeds a member of the parsley family; available in seed or ground form.

cayenne pepper thin-fleshed, long, very-hot red chilli; usually purchased dried and ground.

celeriac tuberous root with brown skin, white flesh and a celery-like flavour.

cheese

cheddar the most common cow's milk 'tasty' cheese; should be aged and hard.

feta a crumbly textured goat's- or sheep's-milk cheese with a sharp, salty taste.

haloumi a firm, cream-coloured sheep's milk cheese matured in brine; can be grilled or fried, briefly, without breaking down.

jarlsberg Norwegian cheese made from cow's milk; firm, with large holes and a mild, nutty taste.

mozzarella a semi-soft cheese with a delicate, fresh taste; has a low melting point and stringy texture when hot.

parmesan a sharp-tasting, dry, hard cheese, made from skimmed or semi-skimmed milk and aged for at least a year.

chicken

breast fillets breast halved, skinned and boned.

drumstick leg with skin intact.

tenderloins the strip of meat lying just under the breast.

thigh cutlets thigh with skin and centre bone intact; sometimes known as a chicken chop.

thigh fillets thigh skinned and boned. wings have skin and bones with a little meat.

chickpeas also called garbanzos, hummus or channa; an irregularly round, sandy-coloured legume.

chillies available in many types and sizes, both fresh and dried. The smaller the chilli, the hotter it is. Wear rubber gloves when handling chillies, as they can burn your skin. Removing seeds and membranes lessens the heat level.

chilli powder the Asian variety is the hottest, made from ground chillies; it can be used as a substitute for fresh chillies in the proportion of ½ teaspoon ground chilli powder to 1 medium chopped fresh chilli.

thai small, medium hot, and bright-red to dark-green in colour.

chinese cabbage also known as peking or napa cabbage, wong bok and petsai, the pale green, crinkly leaves of this elongated cabbage only require brief cooking.

chives related to the onion and leek, with subtle onion flavour.

coconut

milk unsweetened coconut milk available in cans.

shredded thin strips of dried coconut.

cointreau citrus-flavoured liqueur.

cooking oil spray we used a cholesterol-free cooking spray made from canola oil.

coriander

dried a fragrant herb; coriander seeds and ground coriander must never be used to replace fresh coriander or vice versa. The tastes are completely different.

fresh also known as cilantro or chinese parsley; bright-green-leafed herb with a pungent flavour.

corn kernels sometimes called niblets; available canned and frozen.

cornflour also known as cornstarch; used as a thickening agent in cooking.

couscous a fine, grain-like cereal product, made from semolina.

cream we used fresh cream in this book, unless otherwise stated.

114

Also known as pure cream and pouring cream; has no additives unlike commercially thickened cream. Minimum fat content 35%.

soured a thick commercially-cultured soured cream. Minimum fat content 35%.

cumin available both ground and as whole seeds; cumin has a warm, earthy, rather strong flavour.

curry powder a blend of ground spices; choose mild or hot to suit your taste and the recipe.

fennel bulb vegetable, also known as finocchio or anise. Also the name given to dried seeds having a licorice flavour.

fennel seeds dried seeds having a licorice flavour.

fish sauce also called nam pla or nuoc nam; made from pulverised salted fermented fish, mostly anchovies. Has a pungent smell and strong taste; use sparingly.

five-spice powder a fragrant mixture of ground cinnamon, cloves, star anise, sichuan pepper and fennel seeds.

flat-leaf parsley also known as continental parsley or italian parsley.

galangal also known as laos; a dried root that is a member of the ginger family, used whole or ground, having a piquant, peppery flavour.

garam masala a blend of spices based on varying proportions of cardamom, cinnamon, cloves, coriander, fennel and cumin, roasted and ground together. Black pepper and chilli can be added for a hotter version.

garlic, bottled conveniently crushed garlic; available in jars from supermarkets.

gherkins also known as cornichon; young, dark-green cucumbers grown for pickling.

ginger also known as green or root ginger; the thick gnarled root of a tropical plant.

hoisin sauce a thick, sweet and spicy Chinese paste made from salted fermented soy beans, onions and garlic.

ketjap manis also called kecap manis; an Indonesian sweet, thick soy sauce which has sugar and spices added.

lamb

chump chops cut from just above the hind legs to the mid-loin section; can be used whole, for roasting, or cut into chops.

cutlets small, tender rib chop; all fat and gristle from end of bone is removed.

eye of loin a cut derived from a row of loin chops. Once the bone and fat are removed, the larger portion is referred to as the eye of the loin.

fillets tenderloin; the smaller piece of meat from a row of loin chops or cutlets.

forequarter chops from the shoulder end of the sheep. They tend to be fatty so are ideal for braising and casseroles. Leaner forequarter chops can be grilled.

lemongrass a tall, clumping, lemon-smelling and tasting, sharp edged grass; use only the white lower part of each stem.

lemon pepper seasoning a blend of black pepper, lemon, herbs and spices.

lemon thyme a variety of thyme with a lemony fragrance.

mangetout ('eat all') also known as snow peas.

mayonnaise we use whole-egg mayonnaise in our recipes.

mushrooms

button small, cultivated white mushrooms having a delicate, subtle flavour.

flat a rich earthy flavour; sometimes misnamed field mushrooms.

mustard

powder finely ground white (yellow) mustard seeds.

dijon a pale brown, distinctively flavoured fairly mild French mustard.

french plain mild mustard.

wholegrain also known as. seeded A French-style coarse-grain mustard made from crushed mustard seeds and Dijon-style French mustard.

noodles

fried crispy packaged (commonly a 100g packet) already deep-fried.

hokkien also known as stir-fry noodles; fresh wheat flour noodles resembling thick,

yellow-brown spaghetti, needing no pre-cooking before being used.

rice vermicelli also known as rice-flour noodles; made from ground rice. Sold dried, are best either deep-fried or soaked then stir-fried, or used in soups.

soba Japanese dried noodles made of buckwheat flour.

oil

olive mono-unsaturated; made from the pressing of tree-ripened olives. Extra virgin and virgin are the best, obtained from the first pressings of the olive, while extra light or light refers to the taste, not fat levels.

groundnut pressed from ground peanuts; most commonly used in Asian cooking because of its high smoke point.

mustard-seed a mild-tasting oil made from the first pressing of fine yellow mustard seeds; macadamia or hazelnut oil could be used instead.

sesame made from roasted, crushed, white sesame seeds; a flavouring rather than a cooking medium.

onion

spring also known as scallion; an immature onion picked before the bulb has formed, having a long, bright-green edible stalk.

red also known as spanish, red spanish or bermuda onion; a sweet-flavoured, large, purple-red onion.

oyster sauce rich sauce made from oysters and their brine, salt, soy sauce and starches.

pak choy also called pak choi or Chinese chard; has a mild mustard taste and is good braised or in stir-fries. Baby pak choy is also available.

pancetta an Italian salt-cured pork roll, usually cut from the belly; used, chopped, in cooked dishes to add flavours. Bacon can be substituted.

paprika ground dried red bell pepper (capsicum); available sweet or hot.

pepper also known as capsicum or bell pepper; seeds and membranes should be discarded before use.

peppercorns available in black, white, red or green.

green peppercorns soft, unripe berry of pepper plant, usually sold packed in brine.

sichuan peppercorns also known as szechuan or chinese pepper. Small, reddish-brown berries with distinctive peppery-lemon flavour and aroma.

pesto a paste made from fresh basil, oil, garlic, pine nuts and parmesan.

pine nuts also known as pignoli; small, cream-coloured kernels obtained from the cones of different varieties of pine trees.

pistachios pale green, delicately flavoured nut inside hard off-white shells. To peel, soak shelled nuts in boiling water about 5 minutes; drain, then pat dry.

plum sauce a thick, sweet and sour dipping sauce made from plums, vinegar, sugar, chillies and spices.

pork

butterfly steaks skinless, boneless mid-loin chop, split in half and flattened.

fillet skinless, boneless eye-fillet cut from the loin.

loin from pork middle.

spare ribs, american-style well-trimmed mid loin ribs.

radicchio has dark burgundy leaves and strong, bitter taste.

radish a peppery root vegetable related to the mustard plant. The small round red variety is the mildest, it is crisp and juicy and usually eaten raw in salads.

rice

brown natural whole grain.

long grain elongated grain, remains separate when cooked; most popular steaming rice in Asia.

rocket also known as arugula, rugula and rucola; a peppery-tasting green leaf. Also baby rocket.

sambal oelek a salty paste made from ground chillies.

seasoned pepper a packaged preparation of combined black pepper, red capsicum (bell pepper), paprika and garlic.

sesame seeds black and white are the most common of these tiny oval seeds; a good source of calcium.

soy sauce made from fermented soy beans; several variations are available.

sun-dried tomatoes dried tomatoes sometimes bottled in oil.

sweet chilli sauce mild, Thai sauce made from red chillies, sugar, garlic and vinegar.

tabasco sauce brand name of an extremely fiery sauce made from vinegar, hot red peppers and salt.

tamarind sauce if unavailable, soak about 30g dried tamarind in a cup of hot water. Stand 10 minutes and squeeze pulp as dry as possible; use the flavoured water.

tandoori paste Indian blend of hot and fragrant spices including turmeric, paprika, chilli powder, saffron, cardamom and garam masala.

tofu also known as bean curd, an off-white, custard-like product made from the 'milk' of crushed soy beans; comes fresh as soft or firm, and processed as fried or pressed dried sheets. Leftover fresh tofu can be refrigerated in water (which is changed daily) up to four days. Silken tofu refers to the method by which it is made – where it is strained through silk.

tomato

paste triple-concentrated tomato puree used to flavour soups, stews, sauces and casseroles.

ketchup also known as sauce or catsup; a flavoured condiment made from tomatoes, vinegar and spices.

plum also known as egg or roma, smallish, oval-shaped tomatoes.

cherry also known as tiny tim or tom thumb tomatoes; small and round.

tortillas unleavened, round bread; available frozen, fresh or vacuum-packed.

turmeric a member of the ginger family, its root is dried and ground; intensely pungent in taste but not hot.

vinegar

balsamic authentic only from the province of Modena, Italy; made from a regional wine of white trebbiano grapes specially processed then aged in antique wooden casks to give the exquisite pungent flavour.

malt made from fermented malt and beech shavings.

raspberry made from fresh raspberries steeped in a white wine vinegar.

red wine based on fermented red wine.

rice based on fermented rice.

white made from spirit of cane sugar.

white wine based on fermented white wine.

wine we use good-quality dry white and red wines in our recipes.

green ginger beverage 14% alcohol by volume, has the taste of fresh ginger. In cooking, substitute dry (white) vermouth if you prefer.

wakame a dried seaweed used in Japanese cooking; dark greenish-black and extremely rich in calcium, it can be shredded for salads, reconstituted in hot water and eaten as a vegetable or simmered in soups. Available from Japanese and some other Asian food shops; you can use any edible dried seaweed or kelp in its place.

worcestershire sauce a thin, dark-brown spicy sauce.

conversion charts

measures

The cup and spoon measurements used in this book are metric:
one measuring cup holds approximately 250ml; one metric tablespoon holds 20ml; one metric teaspoon holds 5ml.

All cup and spoon measurements are level. The most accurate way of measuring dry ingredients is to weigh them. When measuring liquids, use a clear glass or plastic jug with metric markings. We used large eggs with an average weight of 60g.

WARNING This book may contain recipes for dishes made with raw or lightly cooked eggs. These should be avoided by vulnerable people such as pregnant and nursing mothers, invalids, the elderly, babies and young children.

dry measures

metric	imperial
15g	½oz
30g	1oz
60g	2oz
90g	3oz
125g	4oz (¼lb)
155g	5oz
185g	6oz
220g	7oz
250g	8oz (½lb)
280g	9oz
315g	10oz
345g	11oz
375g	12oz (¾lb)
410g	13oz
440g	14oz
470g	15oz
500g	16oz (1lb)
750g	24oz (1½lb)
1kg	32oz (2lb)

liquid measures

metric	imperial
30ml	1 fl oz
60ml	2 fl oz
100ml	3 fl oz
125ml	4 fl oz
150ml	5 fl oz (¼ pint/1 gill)
190ml	6 fl oz
250ml	8 fl oz
300ml	10 fl oz (½pt)
500ml	16 fl oz
600ml	20 fl oz (1 pint)
1000ml (1 litre)	1¾pints

length measures

metric	imperial
3mm	⅛in
6mm	¼in
1cm	½in
2cm	¾in
2.5cm	1in
5cm	2in
6cm	2½in
8cm	3in
10cm	4in
13cm	5in
15cm	6in
18cm	7in
20cm	8in
23cm	9in
25cm	10in
28cm	11in
30cm	12in (1ft)

oven temperatures

These oven temperatures are only a guide for conventional ovens. For fan-assisted ovens, check the manufacturer's manual.

	°C (Celcius)	°F (Fahrenheit)	gas mark
Very low	120	250	½
Low	150	275-300	1-2
Moderately low	170	325	3
Moderate	180	350-375	4-5
Moderately hot	200	400	6
Hot	220	425-450	7-8
Very hot	240	475	9

index

ACP BOOKS

General manager Christine Whiston
Test kitchen food director Pamela Clark
Editorial director Susan Tomnay
Creative director Hieu Chi Nguyen
Director of sales Brian Cearnes
Marketing manager Bridget Cody
Business analyst Rebecca Varela
Operations manager David Scotto
International rights enquiries Laura Bamford
lbamford@acpuk.com

ACP Books are published by ACP Magazines
a division of PBL Media Pty Limited
Publishing Director, Women's Lifestyle
Pat Ingram
Director of sales, Women's lifestyle
Lynette Phillips
Commercial manager, Women's lifestyle
Seymour Cohen
Marketing director, Women's lifestyle
Matthew Dominello
Public relations manager, Women's lifestyle
Hannah Deveraux
Creative director, Events, Women's lifestyle
Luke Bonnano
Research Director, Women's lifestyle
Justin Stone
PBL Media, Chief Executive officer
Ian Law

Produced by ACP Books, Sydney.
Published by ACP Books, a division of
ACP Magazines Ltd, 54 Park St, Sydney;
GPO Box 4088, Sydney, NSW 2001.
phone (02) 9282 8618 fax (02) 9267 9438.
acpbooks@acpmagazines.com.au
www.acpbooks.com.au
Printed and bound in China.

Australia Distributed by Network Services,
phone +61 2 9282 8777 fax +61 2 9264 3278
networkweb@networkservicescompany.com.au
United Kingdom Distributed by Australian
Consolidated Press (UK),
phone (01604) 642 200 fax (01604) 642 300
books@acpuk.com
New Zealand Distributed by Netlink
Distribution Company,
phone (9) 366 9966 ask@ndc.co.nz
South Africa Distributed by PSD Promotions,
phone (27 11) 392 6065/6/7
fax (27 11) 392 6079/80
orders@psdprom.co.za
Canada Distributed by Publishers Group Canada
phone (800) 663 5714 fax (800) 565 3770
service@raincoast.com

A catalogue record for this book is available from
the British Library.
ISBN 978-1-903777-55-8
© ACP Magazines Ltd 2008
ABN 18 053 273 546